C-545   CAREER EXAMINATION SERIES

This is your
PASSBOOK for...

Rehabilitation Assistant

Test Preparation Study Guide
Questions & Answers

COPYRIGHT NOTICE

This book is SOLELY intended for, is sold ONLY to, and its use is RESTRICTED to individual, bona fide applicants or candidates who qualify by virtue of having seriously filed applications for appropriate license, certificate, professional and/or promotional advancement, higher school matriculation, scholarship, or other legitimate requirements of education and/or governmental authorities.

This book is NOT intended for use, class instruction, tutoring, training, duplication, copying, reprinting, excerption, or adaptation, etc., by:

1) Other publishers
2) Proprietors and/or Instructors of "Coaching" and/or Preparatory Courses
3) Personnel and/or Training Divisions of commercial, industrial, and governmental organizations
4) Schools, colleges, or universities and/or their departments and staffs, including teachers and other personnel
5) Testing Agencies or Bureaus
6) Study groups which seek by the purchase of a single volume to copy and/or duplicate and/or adapt this material for use by the group as a whole without having purchased individual volumes for each of the members of the group
7) Et al.

Such persons would be in violation of appropriate Federal and State statutes.

PROVISION OF LICENSING AGREEMENTS – Recognized educational, commercial, industrial, and governmental institutions and organizations, and others legitimately engaged in educational pursuits, including training, testing, and measurement activities, may address request for a licensing agreement to the copyright owners, who will determine whether, and under what conditions, including fees and charges, the materials in this book may be used them. In other words, a licensing facility exists for the legitimate use of the material in this book on other than an individual basis. However, it is asseverated and affirmed here that the material in this book CANNOT be used without the receipt of the express permission of such a licensing agreement from the Publishers. Inquiries re licensing should be addressed to the company, attention rights and permissions department.

All rights reserved, including the right of reproduction in whole or in part, in any form or by any means, electronic or mechanical, including photocopying, recording, or by any information storage and retrieval system, without permission in writing from the Publisher.

Copyright © 2025 by
National Learning Corporation

212 Michael Drive, Syosset, NY 11791
(516) 921-8888 • www.passbooks.com
E-mail: info@passbooks.com

PASSBOOK® SERIES

THE *PASSBOOK® SERIES* has been created to prepare applicants and candidates for the ultimate academic battlefield – the examination room.

At some time in our lives, each and every one of us may be required to take an examination – for validation, matriculation, admission, qualification, registration, certification, or licensure.

Based on the assumption that every applicant or candidate has met the basic formal educational standards, has taken the required number of courses, and read the necessary texts, the *PASSBOOK® SERIES* furnishes the one special preparation which may assure passing with confidence, instead of failing with insecurity. Examination questions – together with answers – are furnished as the basic vehicle for study so that the mysteries of the examination and its compounding difficulties may be eliminated or diminished by a sure method.

This book is meant to help you pass your examination provided that you qualify and are serious in your objective.

The entire field is reviewed through the huge store of content information which is succinctly presented through a provocative and challenging approach – the question-and-answer method.

A climate of success is established by furnishing the correct answers at the end of each test.

You soon learn to recognize types of questions, forms of questions, and patterns of questioning. You may even begin to anticipate expected outcomes.

You perceive that many questions are repeated or adapted so that you can gain acute insights, which may enable you to score many sure points.

You learn how to confront new questions, or types of questions, and to attack them confidently and work out the correct answers.

You note objectives and emphases, and recognize pitfalls and dangers, so that you may make positive educational adjustments.

Moreover, you are kept fully informed in relation to new concepts, methods, practices, and directions in the field.

You discover that you are actually taking the examination all the time: you are preparing for the examination by "taking" an examination, not by reading extraneous and/or supererogatory textbooks.

In short, this PASSBOOK®, used directedly, should be an important factor in helping you to pass your test.

REHABILITATION ASSISTANT

THE POSITION
As a *REHABILITATION ASSISTANT*, you would work with mentally, emotionally, and developmentally handicapped individuals in a rehabilitation services area. The responsibility of a *Rehabilitation Assistant* is to assist clients, both inpatients and/or outpatients, to achieve personal, social, educational, and vocational growth and maintenance. Utilizing rehabilitation principles and practices, rehabilitation facilities and workshops, you would assist clients to attain their optimal level of functioning. You would be expected to provide service in psychosocial, vocational, residential, and competency training areas.

SUBJECT OF EXAMINATIONS
Written test designed to test for knowledge, skills, and/or abilities in such areas as:
1. Human behavior;
2. Care and understanding of the disabled;
3. Development and implementation of rehabilitation plans; and
4. Record keeping and report preparation.

HOW TO TAKE A TEST

I. YOU MUST PASS AN EXAMINATION

A. WHAT EVERY CANDIDATE SHOULD KNOW

Examination applicants often ask us for help in preparing for the written test. What can I study in advance? What kinds of questions will be asked? How will the test be given? How will the papers be graded?

As an applicant for a civil service examination, you may be wondering about some of these things. Our purpose here is to suggest effective methods of advance study and to describe civil service examinations.

Your chances for success on this examination can be increased if you know how to prepare. Those "pre-examination jitters" can be reduced if you know what to expect. You can even experience an adventure in good citizenship if you know why civil service exams are given.

B. WHY ARE CIVIL SERVICE EXAMINATIONS GIVEN?

Civil service examinations are important to you in two ways. As a citizen, you want public jobs filled by employees who know how to do their work. As a job seeker, you want a fair chance to compete for that job on an equal footing with other candidates. The best-known means of accomplishing this two-fold goal is the competitive examination.

Exams are widely publicized throughout the nation. They may be administered for jobs in federal, state, city, municipal, town or village governments or agencies.

Any citizen may apply, with some limitations, such as the age or residence of applicants. Your experience and education may be reviewed to see whether you meet the requirements for the particular examination. When these requirements exist, they are reasonable and applied consistently to all applicants. Thus, a competitive examination may cause you some uneasiness now, but it is your privilege and safeguard.

C. HOW ARE CIVIL SERVICE EXAMS DEVELOPED?

Examinations are carefully written by trained technicians who are specialists in the field known as "psychological measurement," in consultation with recognized authorities in the field of work that the test will cover. These experts recommend the subject matter areas or skills to be tested; only those knowledges or skills important to your success on the job are included. The most reliable books and source materials available are used as references. Together, the experts and technicians judge the difficulty level of the questions.

Test technicians know how to phrase questions so that the problem is clearly stated. Their ethics do not permit "trick" or "catch" questions. Questions may have been tried out on sample groups, or subjected to statistical analysis, to determine their usefulness.

Written tests are often used in combination with performance tests, ratings of training and experience, and oral interviews. All of these measures combine to form the best-known means of finding the right person for the right job.

II. HOW TO PASS THE WRITTEN TEST

A. NATURE OF THE EXAMINATION

To prepare intelligently for civil service examinations, you should know how they differ from school examinations you have taken. In school you were assigned certain definite pages to read or subjects to cover. The examination questions were quite detailed and usually emphasized memory. Civil service exams, on the other hand, try to discover your present ability to perform the duties of a position, plus your potentiality to learn these duties. In other words, a civil service exam attempts to predict how successful you will be. Questions cover such a broad area that they cannot be as minute and detailed as school exam questions.

In the public service similar kinds of work, or positions, are grouped together in one "class." This process is known as *position-classification*. All the positions in a class are paid according to the salary range for that class. One class title covers all of these positions, and they are all tested by the same examination.

B. FOUR BASIC STEPS

1) Study the announcement

How, then, can you know what subjects to study? Our best answer is: "Learn as much as possible about the class of positions for which you've applied." The exam will test the knowledge, skills and abilities needed to do the work.

Your most valuable source of information about the position you want is the official exam announcement. This announcement lists the training and experience qualifications. Check these standards and apply only if you come reasonably close to meeting them.

The brief description of the position in the examination announcement offers some clues to the subjects which will be tested. Think about the job itself. Review the duties in your mind. Can you perform them, or are there some in which you are rusty? Fill in the blank spots in your preparation.

Many jurisdictions preview the written test in the exam announcement by including a section called "Knowledge and Abilities Required," "Scope of the Examination," or some similar heading. Here you will find out specifically what fields will be tested.

2) Review your own background

Once you learn in general what the position is all about, and what you need to know to do the work, ask yourself which subjects you already know fairly well and which need improvement. You may wonder whether to concentrate on improving your strong areas or on building some background in your fields of weakness. When the announcement has specified "some knowledge" or "considerable knowledge," or has used adjectives like "beginning principles of..." or "advanced ... methods," you can get a clue as to the number and difficulty of questions to be asked in any given field. More questions, and hence broader coverage, would be included for those subjects which are more important in the work. Now weigh your strengths and weaknesses against the job requirements and prepare accordingly.

3) Determine the level of the position

Another way to tell how intensively you should prepare is to understand the level of the job for which you are applying. Is it the entering level? In other words, is this the position in which beginners in a field of work are hired? Or is it an intermediate or advanced level? Sometimes this is indicated by such words as "Junior" or "Senior" in the class title. Other jurisdictions use Roman numerals to designate the level – Clerk I, Clerk II, for example. The word "Supervisor" sometimes appears in the title. If the level is not indicated by the title, check the description of duties. Will you be working under very close supervision, or will you have responsibility for independent decisions in this work?

4) Choose appropriate study materials

Now that you know the subjects to be examined and the relative amount of each subject to be covered, you can choose suitable study materials. For beginning level jobs, or even advanced ones, if you have a pronounced weakness in some aspect of your training, read a modern, standard textbook in that field. Be sure it is up to date and has general coverage. Such books are normally available at your library, and the librarian will be glad to help you locate one. For entry-level positions, questions of appropriate difficulty are chosen – neither highly advanced questions, nor those too simple. Such questions require careful thought but not advanced training.

If the position for which you are applying is technical or advanced, you will read more advanced, specialized material. If you are already familiar with the basic principles of your field, elementary textbooks would waste your time. Concentrate on advanced textbooks and technical periodicals. Think through the concepts and review difficult problems in your field.

These are all general sources. You can get more ideas on your own initiative, following these leads. For example, training manuals and publications of the government agency which employs workers in your field can be useful, particularly for technical and professional positions. A letter or visit to the government department involved may result in more specific study suggestions, and certainly will provide you with a more definite idea of the exact nature of the position you are seeking.

III. KINDS OF TESTS

Tests are used for purposes other than measuring knowledge and ability to perform specified duties. For some positions, it is equally important to test ability to make adjustments to new situations or to profit from training. In others, basic mental abilities not dependent on information are essential. Questions which test these things may not appear as pertinent to the duties of the position as those which test for knowledge and information. Yet they are often highly important parts of a fair examination. For very general questions, it is almost impossible to help you direct your study efforts. What we can do is to point out some of the more common of these general abilities needed in public service positions and describe some typical questions.

1) General information

Broad, general information has been found useful for predicting job success in some kinds of work. This is tested in a variety of ways, from vocabulary lists to questions about current events. Basic background in some field of work, such as sociology or economics, may be sampled in a group of questions. Often these are principles which have become familiar to most persons through exposure rather than through formal training. It is difficult to advise you how to study for these questions; being alert to the world around you is our best suggestion.

2) Verbal ability

An example of an ability needed in many positions is verbal or language ability. Verbal ability is, in brief, the ability to use and understand words. Vocabulary and grammar tests are typical measures of this ability. Reading comprehension or paragraph interpretation questions are common in many kinds of civil service tests. You are given a paragraph of written material and asked to find its central meaning.

3) Numerical ability

Number skills can be tested by the familiar arithmetic problem, by checking paired lists of numbers to see which are alike and which are different, or by interpreting charts and graphs. In the latter test, a graph may be printed in the test booklet which you are asked to use as the basis for answering questions.

4) Observation

A popular test for law-enforcement positions is the observation test. A picture is shown to you for several minutes, then taken away. Questions about the picture test your ability to observe both details and larger elements.

5) Following directions

In many positions in the public service, the employee must be able to carry out written instructions dependably and accurately. You may be given a chart with several columns, each column listing a variety of information. The questions require you to carry out directions involving the information given in the chart.

6) Skills and aptitudes

Performance tests effectively measure some manual skills and aptitudes. When the skill is one in which you are trained, such as typing or shorthand, you can practice. These tests are often very much like those given in business school or high school courses. For many of the other skills and aptitudes, however, no short-time preparation can be made. Skills and abilities natural to you or that you have developed throughout your lifetime are being tested.

Many of the general questions just described provide all the data needed to answer the questions and ask you to use your reasoning ability to find the answers. Your best preparation for these tests, as well as for tests of facts and ideas, is to be at your physical and mental best. You, no doubt, have your own methods of getting into an exam-taking mood and keeping "in shape." The next section lists some ideas on this subject.

IV. KINDS OF QUESTIONS

Only rarely is the "essay" question, which you answer in narrative form, used in civil service tests. Civil service tests are usually of the short-answer type. Full instructions for answering these questions will be given to you at the examination. But in case this is your first experience with short-answer questions and separate answer sheets, here is what you need to know:

1) Multiple-choice Questions

Most popular of the short-answer questions is the "multiple choice" or "best answer" question. It can be used, for example, to test for factual knowledge, ability to solve problems or judgment in meeting situations found at work.

A multiple-choice question is normally one of three types—
- It can begin with an incomplete statement followed by several possible endings. You are to find the one ending which *best* completes the statement, although some of the others may not be entirely wrong.
- It can also be a complete statement in the form of a question which is answered by choosing one of the statements listed.

- It can be in the form of a problem – again you select the best answer.

Here is an example of a multiple-choice question with a discussion which should give you some clues as to the method for choosing the right answer:

When an employee has a complaint about his assignment, the action which will *best* help him overcome his difficulty is to
- A. discuss his difficulty with his coworkers
- B. take the problem to the head of the organization
- C. take the problem to the person who gave him the assignment
- D. say nothing to anyone about his complaint

In answering this question, you should study each of the choices to find which is best. Consider choice "A" – Certainly an employee may discuss his complaint with fellow employees, but no change or improvement can result, and the complaint remains unresolved. Choice "B" is a poor choice since the head of the organization probably does not know what assignment you have been given, and taking your problem to him is known as "going over the head" of the supervisor. The supervisor, or person who made the assignment, is the person who can clarify it or correct any injustice. Choice "C" is, therefore, correct. To say nothing, as in choice "D," is unwise. Supervisors have and interest in knowing the problems employees are facing, and the employee is seeking a solution to his problem.

2) True/False Questions

The "true/false" or "right/wrong" form of question is sometimes used. Here a complete statement is given. Your job is to decide whether the statement is right or wrong.

SAMPLE: A roaming cell-phone call to a nearby city costs less than a non-roaming call to a distant city.

This statement is wrong, or false, since roaming calls are more expensive.

This is not a complete list of all possible question forms, although most of the others are variations of these common types. You will always get complete directions for answering questions. Be sure you understand *how* to mark your answers – ask questions until you do.

V. RECORDING YOUR ANSWERS

Computer terminals are used more and more today for many different kinds of exams.

For an examination with very few applicants, you may be told to record your answers in the test booklet itself. Separate answer sheets are much more common. If this separate answer sheet is to be scored by machine – and this is often the case – it is highly important that you mark your answers correctly in order to get credit.

An electronic scoring machine is often used in civil service offices because of the speed with which papers can be scored. Machine-scored answer sheets must be marked with a pencil, which will be given to you. This pencil has a high graphite content which responds to the electronic scoring machine. As a matter of fact, stray dots may register as answers, so do not let your pencil rest on the answer sheet while you are pondering the correct answer. Also, if your pencil lead breaks or is otherwise defective, ask for another.

Since the answer sheet will be dropped in a slot in the scoring machine, be careful not to bend the corners or get the paper crumpled.

The answer sheet normally has five vertical columns of numbers, with 30 numbers to a column. These numbers correspond to the question numbers in your test booklet. After each number, going across the page are four or five pairs of dotted lines. These short dotted lines have small letters or numbers above them. The first two pairs may also have a "T" or "F" above the letters. This indicates that the first two pairs only are to be used if the questions are of the true-false type. If the questions are multiple choice, disregard the "T" and "F" and pay attention only to the small letters or numbers.

Answer your questions in the manner of the sample that follows:

32. The largest city in the United States is
    A. Washington, D.C.
    B. New York City
    C. Chicago
    D. Detroit
    E. San Francisco

1) Choose the answer you think is best. (New York City is the largest, so "B" is correct.)
2) Find the row of dotted lines numbered the same as the question you are answering. (Find row number 32)
3) Find the pair of dotted lines corresponding to the answer. (Find the pair of lines under the mark "B.")
4) Make a solid black mark between the dotted lines.

VI. BEFORE THE TEST

Common sense will help you find procedures to follow to get ready for an examination. Too many of us, however, overlook these sensible measures. Indeed, nervousness and fatigue have been found to be the most serious reasons why applicants fail to do their best on civil service tests. Here is a list of reminders:

- Begin your preparation early – Don't wait until the last minute to go scurrying around for books and materials or to find out what the position is all about.
- Prepare continuously – An hour a night for a week is better than an all-night cram session. This has been definitely established. What is more, a night a week for a month will return better dividends than crowding your study into a shorter period of time.
- Locate the place of the exam – You have been sent a notice telling you when and where to report for the examination. If the location is in a different town or otherwise unfamiliar to you, it would be well to inquire the best route and learn something about the building.
- Relax the night before the test – Allow your mind to rest. Do not study at all that night. Plan some mild recreation or diversion; then go to bed early and get a good night's sleep.
- Get up early enough to make a leisurely trip to the place for the test – This way unforeseen events, traffic snarls, unfamiliar buildings, etc. will not upset you.
- Dress comfortably – A written test is not a fashion show. You will be known by number and not by name, so wear something comfortable.

- Leave excess paraphernalia at home – Shopping bags and odd bundles will get in your way. You need bring only the items mentioned in the official notice you received; usually everything you need is provided. Do not bring reference books to the exam. They will only confuse those last minutes and be taken away from you when in the test room.
- Arrive somewhat ahead of time – If because of transportation schedules you must get there very early, bring a newspaper or magazine to take your mind off yourself while waiting.
- Locate the examination room – When you have found the proper room, you will be directed to the seat or part of the room where you will sit. Sometimes you are given a sheet of instructions to read while you are waiting. Do not fill out any forms until you are told to do so; just read them and be prepared.
- Relax and prepare to listen to the instructions
- If you have any physical problem that may keep you from doing your best, be sure to tell the test administrator. If you are sick or in poor health, you really cannot do your best on the exam. You can come back and take the test some other time.

VII. AT THE TEST

The day of the test is here and you have the test booklet in your hand. The temptation to get going is very strong. Caution! There is more to success than knowing the right answers. You must know how to identify your papers and understand variations in the type of short-answer question used in this particular examination. Follow these suggestions for maximum results from your efforts:

1) Cooperate with the monitor

The test administrator has a duty to create a situation in which you can be as much at ease as possible. He will give instructions, tell you when to begin, check to see that you are marking your answer sheet correctly, and so on. He is not there to guard you, although he will see that your competitors do not take unfair advantage. He wants to help you do your best.

2) Listen to all instructions

Don't jump the gun! Wait until you understand all directions. In most civil service tests you get more time than you need to answer the questions. So don't be in a hurry. Read each word of instructions until you clearly understand the meaning. Study the examples, listen to all announcements and follow directions. Ask questions if you do not understand what to do.

3) Identify your papers

Civil service exams are usually identified by number only. You will be assigned a number; you must not put your name on your test papers. Be sure to copy your number correctly. Since more than one exam may be given, copy your exact examination title.

4) Plan your time

Unless you are told that a test is a "speed" or "rate of work" test, speed itself is usually not important. Time enough to answer all the questions will be provided, but this does not mean that you have all day. An overall time limit has been set. Divide the total time (in minutes) by the number of questions to determine the approximate time you have for each question.

5) Do not linger over difficult questions

If you come across a difficult question, mark it with a paper clip (useful to have along) and come back to it when you have been through the booklet. One caution if you do this – be sure to skip a number on your answer sheet as well. Check often to be sure that you have not lost your place and that you are marking in the row numbered the same as the question you are answering.

6) Read the questions

Be sure you know what the question asks! Many capable people are unsuccessful because they failed to *read* the questions correctly.

7) Answer all questions

Unless you have been instructed that a penalty will be deducted for incorrect answers, it is better to guess than to omit a question.

8) Speed tests

It is often better NOT to guess on speed tests. It has been found that on timed tests people are tempted to spend the last few seconds before time is called in marking answers at random – without even reading them – in the hope of picking up a few extra points. To discourage this practice, the instructions may warn you that your score will be "corrected" for guessing. That is, a penalty will be applied. The incorrect answers will be deducted from the correct ones, or some other penalty formula will be used.

9) Review your answers

If you finish before time is called, go back to the questions you guessed or omitted to give them further thought. Review other answers if you have time.

10) Return your test materials

If you are ready to leave before others have finished or time is called, take ALL your materials to the monitor and leave quietly. Never take any test material with you. The monitor can discover whose papers are not complete, and taking a test booklet may be grounds for disqualification.

VIII. EXAMINATION TECHNIQUES

1) Read the general instructions carefully. These are usually printed on the first page of the exam booklet. As a rule, these instructions refer to the timing of the examination; the fact that you should not start work until the signal and must stop work at a signal, etc. If there are any *special* instructions, such as a choice of questions to be answered, make sure that you note this instruction carefully.

2) When you are ready to start work on the examination, that is as soon as the signal has been given, read the instructions to each question booklet, underline any key words or phrases, such as *least, best, outline, describe* and the like. In this way you will tend to answer as requested rather than discover on reviewing your paper that you *listed without describing*, that you selected the *worst* choice rather than the *best* choice, etc.

3) If the examination is of the objective or multiple-choice type – that is, each question will also give a series of possible answers: A, B, C or D, and you are called upon to select the best answer and write the letter next to that answer on your answer paper – it is advisable to start answering each question in turn. There may be anywhere from 50 to 100 such questions in the three or four hours allotted and you can see how much time would be taken if you read through all the questions before beginning to answer any. Furthermore, if you come across a question or group of questions which you know would be difficult to answer, it would undoubtedly affect your handling of all the other questions.

4) If the examination is of the essay type and contains but a few questions, it is a moot point as to whether you should read all the questions before starting to answer any one. Of course, if you are given a choice – say five out of seven and the like – then it is essential to read all the questions so you can eliminate the two that are most difficult. If, however, you are asked to answer all the questions, there may be danger in trying to answer the easiest one first because you may find that you will spend too much time on it. The best technique is to answer the first question, then proceed to the second, etc.

5) Time your answers. Before the exam begins, write down the time it started, then add the time allowed for the examination and write down the time it must be completed, then divide the time available somewhat as follows:
    - If 3-1/2 hours are allowed, that would be 210 minutes. If you have 80 objective-type questions, that would be an average of 2-1/2 minutes per question. Allow yourself no more than 2 minutes per question, or a total of 160 minutes, which will permit about 50 minutes to review.
    - If for the time allotment of 210 minutes there are 7 essay questions to answer, that would average about 30 minutes a question. Give yourself only 25 minutes per question so that you have about 35 minutes to review.

6) The most important instruction is to *read each question* and make sure you know what is wanted. The second most important instruction is to *time yourself properly* so that you answer every question. The third most important instruction is to *answer every question*. Guess if you have to but include something for each question. Remember that you will receive no credit for a blank and will probably receive some credit if you write something in answer to an essay question. If you guess a letter – say "B" for a multiple-choice question – you may have guessed right. If you leave a blank as an answer to a multiple-choice question, the examiners may respect your feelings but it will not add a point to your score. Some exams may penalize you for wrong answers, so in such cases *only*, you may not want to guess unless you have some basis for your answer.

7) Suggestions
    a. Objective-type questions
        1. Examine the question booklet for proper sequence of pages and questions
        2. Read all instructions carefully
        3. Skip any question which seems too difficult; return to it after all other questions have been answered
        4. Apportion your time properly; do not spend too much time on any single question or group of questions

5. Note and underline key words – *all, most, fewest, least, best, worst, same, opposite*, etc.
6. Pay particular attention to negatives
7. Note unusual option, e.g., unduly long, short, complex, different or similar in content to the body of the question
8. Observe the use of "hedging" words – *probably, may, most likely*, etc.
9. Make sure that your answer is put next to the same number as the question
10. Do not second-guess unless you have good reason to believe the second answer is definitely more correct
11. Cross out original answer if you decide another answer is more accurate; do not erase until you are ready to hand your paper in
12. Answer all questions; guess unless instructed otherwise
13. Leave time for review

  b. Essay questions
1. Read each question carefully
2. Determine exactly what is wanted. Underline key words or phrases.
3. Decide on outline or paragraph answer
4. Include many different points and elements unless asked to develop any one or two points or elements
5. Show impartiality by giving pros and cons unless directed to select one side only
6. Make and write down any assumptions you find necessary to answer the questions
7. Watch your English, grammar, punctuation and choice of words
8. Time your answers; don't crowd material

8) Answering the essay question

Most essay questions can be answered by framing the specific response around several key words or ideas. Here are a few such key words or ideas:

M's: manpower, materials, methods, money, management
P's: purpose, program, policy, plan, procedure, practice, problems, pitfalls, personnel, public relations

  a. Six basic steps in handling problems:
1. Preliminary plan and background development
2. Collect information, data and facts
3. Analyze and interpret information, data and facts
4. Analyze and develop solutions as well as make recommendations
5. Prepare report and sell recommendations
6. Install recommendations and follow up effectiveness

  b. Pitfalls to avoid
1. *Taking things for granted* – A statement of the situation does not necessarily imply that each of the elements is necessarily true; for example, a complaint may be invalid and biased so that all that can be taken for granted is that a complaint has been registered

2. *Considering only one side of a situation* – Wherever possible, indicate several alternatives and then point out the reasons you selected the best one
3. *Failing to indicate follow up* – Whenever your answer indicates action on your part, make certain that you will take proper follow-up action to see how successful your recommendations, procedures or actions turn out to be
4. *Taking too long in answering any single question* – Remember to time your answers properly

IX. AFTER THE TEST

Scoring procedures differ in detail among civil service jurisdictions although the general principles are the same. Whether the papers are hand-scored or graded by machine we have described, they are nearly always graded by number. That is, the person who marks the paper knows only the number – never the name – of the applicant. Not until all the papers have been graded will they be matched with names. If other tests, such as training and experience or oral interview ratings have been given, scores will be combined. Different parts of the examination usually have different weights. For example, the written test might count 60 percent of the final grade, and a rating of training and experience 40 percent. In many jurisdictions, veterans will have a certain number of points added to their grades.

After the final grade has been determined, the names are placed in grade order and an eligible list is established. There are various methods for resolving ties between those who get the same final grade – probably the most common is to place first the name of the person whose application was received first. Job offers are made from the eligible list in the order the names appear on it. You will be notified of your grade and your rank as soon as all these computations have been made. This will be done as rapidly as possible.

People who are found to meet the requirements in the announcement are called "eligibles." Their names are put on a list of eligible candidates. An eligible's chances of getting a job depend on how high he stands on this list and how fast agencies are filling jobs from the list.

When a job is to be filled from a list of eligibles, the agency asks for the names of people on the list of eligibles for that job. When the civil service commission receives this request, it sends to the agency the names of the three people highest on this list. Or, if the job to be filled has specialized requirements, the office sends the agency the names of the top three persons who meet these requirements from the general list.

The appointing officer makes a choice from among the three people whose names were sent to him. If the selected person accepts the appointment, the names of the others are put back on the list to be considered for future openings.

That is the rule in hiring from all kinds of eligible lists, whether they are for typist, carpenter, chemist, or something else. For every vacancy, the appointing officer has his choice of any one of the top three eligibles on the list. This explains why the person whose name is on top of the list sometimes does not get an appointment when some of the persons lower on the list do. If the appointing officer chooses the second or third eligible, the No. 1 eligible does not get a job at once, but stays on the list until he is appointed or the list is terminated.

X. HOW TO PASS THE INTERVIEW TEST

The examination for which you applied requires an oral interview test. You have already taken the written test and you are now being called for the interview test – the final part of the formal examination.

You may think that it is not possible to prepare for an interview test and that there are no procedures to follow during an interview. Our purpose is to point out some things you can do in advance that will help you and some good rules to follow and pitfalls to avoid while you are being interviewed.

What is an interview supposed to test?

The written examination is designed to test the technical knowledge and competence of the candidate; the oral is designed to evaluate intangible qualities, not readily measured otherwise, and to establish a list showing the relative fitness of each candidate – as measured against his competitors – for the position sought. Scoring is not on the basis of "right" and "wrong," but on a sliding scale of values ranging from "not passable" to "outstanding." As a matter of fact, it is possible to achieve a relatively low score without a single "incorrect" answer because of evident weakness in the qualities being measured.

Occasionally, an examination may consist entirely of an oral test – either an individual or a group oral. In such cases, information is sought concerning the technical knowledges and abilities of the candidate, since there has been no written examination for this purpose. More commonly, however, an oral test is used to supplement a written examination.

Who conducts interviews?

The composition of oral boards varies among different jurisdictions. In nearly all, a representative of the personnel department serves as chairman. One of the members of the board may be a representative of the department in which the candidate would work. In some cases, "outside experts" are used, and, frequently, a businessman or some other representative of the general public is asked to serve. Labor and management or other special groups may be represented. The aim is to occure the services of experts in the appropriate field.

However the board is composed, it is a good idea (and not at all improper or unethical) to ascertain in advance of the interview who the members are and what groups they represent. When you are introduced to them, you will have some idea of their backgrounds and interests, and at least you will not stutter and stammer over their names.

What should be done before the interview?

While knowledge about the board members is useful and takes some of the surprise element out of the interview, there is other preparation which is more substantive. It *is* possible to prepare for an oral interview – in several ways:

1) Keep a copy of your application and review it carefully before the interview

This may be the only document before the oral board, and the starting point of the interview. Know what education and experience you have listed there, and the sequence and dates of all of it. Sometimes the board will ask you to review the highlights of your experience for them; you should not have to hem and haw doing it.

2) Study the class specification and the examination announcement

Usually, the oral board has one or both of these to guide them. The qualities, characteristics or knowledges required by the position sought are stated in these documents. They offer valuable clues as to the nature of the oral interview. For example, if the job involves supervisory responsibilities, the announcement will usually indicate that knowledge of modern supervisory methods and the qualifications of the candidate as a supervisor will be tested. If so, you can expect such questions, frequently in the form of a hypothetical situation which you are expected to solve. NEVER go into an oral without knowledge of the duties and responsibilities of the job you seek.

3) Think through each qualification required

Try to visualize the kind of questions you would ask if you were a board member. How well could you answer them? Try especially to appraise your own knowledge and background in each area, *measured against the job sought*, and identify any areas in which you are weak. Be critical and realistic – do not flatter yourself.

4) Do some general reading in areas in which you feel you may be weak

For example, if the job involves supervision and your past experience has NOT, some general reading in supervisory methods and practices, particularly in the field of human relations, might be useful. Do NOT study agency procedures or detailed manuals. The oral board will be testing your understanding and capacity, not your memory.

5) Get a good night's sleep and watch your general health and mental attitude

You will want a clear head at the interview. Take care of a cold or any other minor ailment, and of course, no hangovers.

What should be done on the day of the interview?

Now comes the day of the interview itself. Give yourself plenty of time to get there. Plan to arrive somewhat ahead of the scheduled time, particularly if your appointment is in the fore part of the day. If a previous candidate fails to appear, the board might be ready for you a bit early. By early afternoon an oral board is almost invariably behind schedule if there are many candidates, and you may have to wait. Take along a book or magazine to read, or your application to review, but leave any extraneous material in the waiting room when you go in for your interview. In any event, relax and compose yourself.

The matter of dress is important. The board is forming impressions about you – from your experience, your manners, your attitude, and your appearance. Give your personal appearance careful attention. Dress your best, but not your flashiest. Choose conservative, appropriate clothing, and be sure it is immaculate. This is a business interview, and your appearance should indicate that you regard it as such. Besides, being well groomed and properly dressed will help boost your confidence.

Sooner or later, someone will call your name and escort you into the interview room. *This is it.* From here on you are on your own. It is too late for any more preparation. But remember, you asked for this opportunity to prove your fitness, and you are here because your request was granted.

What happens when you go in?

The usual sequence of events will be as follows: The clerk (who is often the board stenographer) will introduce you to the chairman of the oral board, who will introduce you to the other members of the board. Acknowledge the introductions before you sit down. Do not be surprised if you find a microphone facing you or a stenotypist sitting by. Oral interviews are usually recorded in the event of an appeal or other review.

Usually the chairman of the board will open the interview by reviewing the highlights of your education and work experience from your application – primarily for the benefit of the other members of the board, as well as to get the material into the record. Do not interrupt or comment unless there is an error or significant misinterpretation; if that is the case, do not hesitate. But do not quibble about insignificant matters. Also, he will usually ask you some question about your education, experience or your present job – partly to get you to start talking and to establish the interviewing "rapport." He may start the actual questioning, or turn it over to one of the other members. Frequently, each member undertakes the questioning on a particular area, one in which he is perhaps most competent, so you can expect each member to participate in the examination. Because time is limited, you may also expect some rather abrupt switches in the direction the questioning takes, so do not be upset by it. Normally, a board member will not pursue a single line of questioning unless he discovers a particular strength or weakness.

After each member has participated, the chairman will usually ask whether any member has any further questions, then will ask you if you have anything you wish to add. Unless you are expecting this question, it may floor you. Worse, it may start you off on an extended, extemporaneous speech. The board is not usually seeking more information. The question is principally to offer you a last opportunity to present further qualifications or to indicate that you have nothing to add. So, if you feel that a significant qualification or characteristic has been overlooked, it is proper to point it out in a sentence or so. Do not compliment the board on the thoroughness of their examination – they have been sketchy, and you know it. If you wish, merely say, "No thank you, I have nothing further to add." This is a point where you can "talk yourself out" of a good impression or fail to present an important bit of information. Remember, *you close the interview yourself*.

The chairman will then say, "That is all, Mr. _____, thank you." Do not be startled; the interview is over, and quicker than you think. Thank him, gather your belongings and take your leave. Save your sigh of relief for the other side of the door.

How to put your best foot forward

Throughout this entire process, you may feel that the board individually and collectively is trying to pierce your defenses, seek out your hidden weaknesses and embarrass and confuse you. Actually, this is not true. They are obliged to make an appraisal of your qualifications for the job you are seeking, and they want to see you in your best light. Remember, they must interview all candidates and a non-cooperative candidate may become a failure in spite of their best efforts to bring out his qualifications. Here are 15 suggestions that will help you:

1) Be natural – Keep your attitude confident, not cocky

If you are not confident that you can do the job, do not expect the board to be. Do not apologize for your weaknesses, try to bring out your strong points. The board is interested in a positive, not negative, presentation. Cockiness will antagonize any board member and make him wonder if you are covering up a weakness by a false show of strength.

2) Get comfortable, but don't lounge or sprawl

Sit erectly but not stiffly. A careless posture may lead the board to conclude that you are careless in other things, or at least that you are not impressed by the importance of the occasion. Either conclusion is natural, even if incorrect. Do not fuss with your clothing, a pencil or an ashtray. Your hands may occasionally be useful to emphasize a point; do not let them become a point of distraction.

3) Do not wisecrack or make small talk

This is a serious situation, and your attitude should show that you consider it as such. Further, the time of the board is limited – they do not want to waste it, and neither should you.

4) Do not exaggerate your experience or abilities

In the first place, from information in the application or other interviews and sources, the board may know more about you than you think. Secondly, you probably will not get away with it. An experienced board is rather adept at spotting such a situation, so do not take the chance.

5) If you know a board member, do not make a point of it, yet do not hide it

Certainly you are not fooling him, and probably not the other members of the board. Do not try to take advantage of your acquaintanceship – it will probably do you little good.

6) Do not dominate the interview

Let the board do that. They will give you the clues – do not assume that you have to do all the talking. Realize that the board has a number of questions to ask you, and do not try to take up all the interview time by showing off your extensive knowledge of the answer to the first one.

7) Be attentive

You only have 20 minutes or so, and you should keep your attention at its sharpest throughout. When a member is addressing a problem or question to you, give him your undivided attention. Address your reply principally to him, but do not exclude the other board members.

8) Do not interrupt

A board member may be stating a problem for you to analyze. He will ask you a question when the time comes. Let him state the problem, and wait for the question.

9) Make sure you understand the question

Do not try to answer until you are sure what the question is. If it is not clear, restate it in your own words or ask the board member to clarify it for you. However, do not haggle about minor elements.

10) Reply promptly but not hastily

A common entry on oral board rating sheets is "candidate responded readily," or "candidate hesitated in replies." Respond as promptly and quickly as you can, but do not jump to a hasty, ill-considered answer.

11) Do not be peremptory in your answers

A brief answer is proper – but do not fire your answer back. That is a losing game from your point of view. The board member can probably ask questions much faster than you can answer them.

12) Do not try to create the answer you think the board member wants

He is interested in what kind of mind you have and how it works – not in playing games. Furthermore, he can usually spot this practice and will actually grade you down on it.

13) Do not switch sides in your reply merely to agree with a board member

Frequently, a member will take a contrary position merely to draw you out and to see if you are willing and able to defend your point of view. Do not start a debate, yet do not surrender a good position. If a position is worth taking, it is worth defending.

14) Do not be afraid to admit an error in judgment if you are shown to be wrong

The board knows that you are forced to reply without any opportunity for careful consideration. Your answer may be demonstrably wrong. If so, admit it and get on with the interview.

15) Do not dwell at length on your present job

The opening question may relate to your present assignment. Answer the question but do not go into an extended discussion. You are being examined for a *new* job, not your present one. As a matter of fact, try to phrase ALL your answers in terms of the job for which you are being examined.

Basis of Rating

Probably you will forget most of these "do's" and "don'ts" when you walk into the oral interview room. Even remembering them all will not ensure you a passing grade. Perhaps you did not have the qualifications in the first place. But remembering them will help you to put your best foot forward, without treading on the toes of the board members.

Rumor and popular opinion to the contrary notwithstanding, an oral board wants you to make the best appearance possible. They know you are under pressure – but they also want to see how you respond to it as a guide to what your reaction would be under the pressures of the job you seek. They will be influenced by the degree of poise you display, the personal traits you show and the manner in which you respond.

ABOUT THIS BOOK

This book contains tests divided into Examination Sections. Go through each test, answering every question in the margin. We have also attached a sample answer sheet at the back of the book that can be removed and used. At the end of each test look at the answer key and check your answers. On the ones you got wrong, look at the right answer choice and learn. Do not fill in the answers first. Do not memorize the questions and answers, but understand the answer and principles involved. On your test, the questions will likely be different from the samples. Questions are changed and new ones added. If you understand these past questions you should have success with any changes that arise. Tests may consist of several types of questions. We have additional books on each subject should more study be advisable or necessary for you. Finally, the more you study, the better prepared you will be. This book is intended to be the last thing you study before you walk into the examination room. Prior study of relevant texts is also recommended. NLC publishes some of these in our Fundamental Series. Knowledge and good sense are important factors in passing your exam. Good luck also helps. So now study this Passbook, absorb the material contained within and take that knowledge into the examination. Then do your best to pass that exam.

EXAMINATION SECTION

EXAMINATION SECTION
TEST 1

DIRECTIONS: Each question or incomplete statement is followed by several suggested answers or completions. Select the one that BEST answers the question or completes the statement. *PRINT THE LETTER OF THE CORRECT ANSWER IN THE SPACE AT THE RIGHT.*

1. Of the following, the FIRST step in the vocational guidance of the physically handicapped is the determination of the subject's

   A. emotional and social attitudes
   B. previous employment history
   C. specific physical limitations
   D. none of the above

   1.____

2. Of the following, the type of job that might BEST be learned by on-the-job training, while receiving physical restoration and rehabilitation in a hospital, is

   A. medical stenography
   B. medical technology
   C. physical therapy
   D. telephone switchboard operation

   2.____

3. In considering broad areas of employment for many of the physically handicapped individuals, the group of occupations that should be explored for increasing employment opportunities at this time is the

   A. professional   B. service
   C. skilled   D. unskilled

   3.____

4. The group of occupations in which all the jobs involve the performance of simple duties, quickly learned and requiring little or no independent judgment, is the

   A. clerical   B. semi-skilled
   C. service   D. unskilled

   4.____

5. The *Dictionary of Occupational Titles* is published by the

   A. Psychological Corporation
   B. U.S. Department of Commerce
   C. U.S. Department of Health, Education and Welfare
   D. U.S. Department of Labor

   5.____

6. The number of job titles included in the *Dictionary of Occupational Titles* is APPROXIMATELY

   A. 10,000   B. 30,000   C. 60,000   D. 100,000

   6.____

7. The professional and managerial occupations in the *Dictionary of Occupational Titles* range from the occupational code 0-00.00 through

   A. 0-39.99   B. 0-99.99   C. 1-49.99   D. 1-89.99

   7.____

8. A rehabilitation counselor may be characterized as an assembler and interpreter of information which will aid individuals in making decisions.
The one of the following which is LEAST likely to be considered one of his functions is

   A. constructing and administering tests designed to measure vocational aptitudes
   B. familiarizing himself with the physical condition of the patient
   C. securing and evaluating information concerning abilities, education, vocational training, and experience
   D. studying occupational information and comparing occupational requirements

9. Throughout the counseling procedure, the rehabilitation counselor should be in a position to discuss occupational information with the client.
The one of the following which he would be LEAST likely to discuss in this process is

   A. interview procedures and techniques
   B. labor market information and trends
   C. nature of the work
   D. requirements and methods of entering the job

10. The counselor learns that a client had served in the U.S. Navy during World War II and has a detailed knowledge of fire control instruments aboard ship.
One of the civilian occupations that should, therefore, be recommended for further exploration is

   A. accountant
   B. draftsman
   C. medical technician
   D. personnel man

11. The one of the following employments which the counselor should NOT recommend to an asthmatic patient is

   A. bank teller
   B. heat treater
   C. statistical clerk
   D. watch repairer

12. *The Fact Book on Manpower,* published by the Bureau of Labor Statistics, presents a

   A. guide on the physical demands of existing job titles
   B. series of tables and graphic information on the working population
   C. statistical analyses of manpower shortages and surpluses
   D. tabular and pictorial descriptions of jobs available for the handicapped

13. The intensive and direct method of obtaining the pertinent facts about jobs is referred to as job

   A. analysis
   B. classification
   C. finding
   D. none of the above

14. The literature in the field of occupations USUALLY classifies a group of tasks performed by one person as a(n)

   A. job
   B. occupation
   C. position
   D. none of the above

15. Of the following, the kind of information which has the LEAST relevancy in making a job analysis is

   A. economic   B. physical   C. social   D. technical

16. Of the following, the kind of test LEAST likely to be significant in determining achievement in the various trades is

    A. manipulation B. performance
    C. picture D. written

17. It has been the experience of rehabilitation counselors that failure on the job by a disabled worker is MOST likely to be caused by

    A. emotional maladjustment B. insufficient intelligence
    C. lack of skills D. physical incapacities

18. When a certain test measures certain qualities consistently, the test is said to be

    A. objective B. reliable C. subjective D. valid

19. The point in a distribution of scores above which and below which lie an equal number of scores is USUALLY referred to as the

    A. mean B. median
    C. mode D. arithmetic average

20. That point on the normal distribution curve which is the greatest distance from the base line represents a measure of ability characterized as

    A. average B. below average
    C. genius D. superior

21. In statistics, the graphic representation of distributions from cumulative frequencies is called the

    A. frequency polygon B. histogram
    C. ogive D. parabolic curve

22. A frequency distribution is said to be *skewed* if the measures tend to

    A. be found at any point along a continuous linear scale
    B. be symmetrical, with one broad smooth hump in the middle, tapering off gradually at either end
    C. make a frequency curve in which the two halves of the figure coincide
    D. pile up at one end or the other of the range of measure

23. One measure of variability is the semi-interquartile range of Q. This measure is half of the distance between which of the following percentile scores?

    A. 100th and 25th B. 75th and 25th
    C. 75th and 50th D. 50th and 25th

24. The standard deviation of a distribution may be defined as the

    A. percentiles of the total area which are included between the mean ordinate and the ordinates at sigma-distances from the mean
    B. square of the absolute amount of deviation from the mean that is exceeded by half of the measures in the distribution
    C. square root of the mean of the deviations from the mean
    D. square root of the mean of the squared deviations from the mean

25. As part of a vocational guidance program, a group of patients has been given two standardized tests.
If the relative rank of the patients is the same on both tests, the coefficient of correlation can be represented as

A. .0 B. .50 C. 1.0 D. 2.0

KEY (CORRECT ANSWERS)

1. C
2. D
3. B
4. D
5. D

6. B
7. B
8. A
9. A
10. B

11. B
12. B
13. A
14. C
15. C

16. D
17. A
18. B
19. B
20. A

21. C
22. D
23. B
24. D
25. C

TEST 2

DIRECTIONS: Each question or incomplete statement is followed by several suggested answers or completions. Select the one that BEST answers the question or completes the statement. *PRINT THE LETTER OF THE CORRECT ANSWER IN THE SPACE AT THE RIGHT.*

1. Of the following, the test which requires the use of apparatus is the   1.____

    A. Minnesota Paper Form Board
    B. Minnesota Spatial Relations Test
    C. Ohio State Psychological Test
    D. Woody McCall Arithmetic Test

2. Of the following, the test that should NOT be used with persons who are unable to speak or read English proficiently is   2.____

    A. Army Alpha - Revised   B. Army Beta
    C. Wechsler-Bellevue   D. none of the above

3. The Minnesota Clerical Test is a test of   3.____

    A. computation, spelling, coding, cancellation, and classification
    B. general mental ability, weighted in favor of the person who possesses office aptitudes or skills
    C. simple computations - additions, subtractions, multiplications, and divisions
    D. speed and accuracy in checking 200 pairs of numbers and 200 pairs of names

4. The Crawford Small Parts Dexterity Test measures   4.____

    A. coordinated manipulation with both hands
    B. fine eye-hand coordination
    C. hand and arm movement
    D. manipulation of wrenches and screwdrivers

5. In the Wechsler-Bellevue Intelligence Scale,   5.____

    A. all instructions to the child are given in pantomine
    B. five tests are verbal and five are nonverbal performance tests
    C. nonpictorial diagrams are used in a series-completion type of item
    D. verbal ability is separated from numerical ability

6. The Minnesota Multiphasic Personality Inventory is a diagnostic test measuring, in part,   6.____

    A. attitudes of pupils toward school
    B. family relations
    C. masculinity and femininity
    D. study skills

7. The Thematic Apperception Test is a   7.____

    A. measure of aptitude for the appreciation or production of art
    B. measure of interests and preferences in a variety of occupations
    C. reading test based on interpretation of difficult paragraphs
    D. set of thirty-one picture cards

8. A broad survey of the many established and experimental methods of appraising personality through projections elicited from the individual is contained in *Projective Techniques,* a book by

   A. John E. Bell
   B. Florence L. Goodenough
   C. Quinn McNemar
   D. Lewis M. Terman

9. The one of the following which is NOT a book written by Dr. Arnold Gesell and staff of the Yale Clinic of Child Development is

   A. INFANT AND CHILD IN THE CULTURE OF TODAY
   B. THE CHILD FROM FIVE TO TEN
   C. THE FIRST FIVE YEARS OF LIFE
   D. THE MEASUREMENT OF INTELLIGENCE OF INFANTS AND YOUNG CHILDREN

10. A basic book in the field of vocational guidance, discussing the relationship between interest, intelligence, and personality tests, with illustrations of how the three should be utilized in counseling was written by

    A. Roger M. Bellows
    B. David Rapaport
    C. Edwin K. Strong, Jr.
    D. Robert L. Thorndike

Questions 11-20.

DIRECTIONS: Column I lists the names of ten individuals who have been prominent in the field of rehabilitation. Each of them can be properly matched with one of the items listed in Column II. Write in the corresponding space at the right the letter in front of the item in Column II with which each name in Column I is MOST closely associated.

COLUMN I	COLUMN II	
11. Barker	A. American Heart Association	11. ____
12. Carlson	B. American Rehabilitation Committee	12. ____
13. DiMichael	C. Arthritis	13. ____
14. Kessler	D. Blindness	14. ____
15. Lowenfeld	E. Cerebral Palsy	15. ____
16. Menninger	F. Facial Disfigurement	16. ____
17. Rusk	G. Hard of Hearing	17. ____
18. Seidenfeld	H. Havestraw Rehabilitation	18. ____
19. Switzer	I. Infantile Paralysis	19. ____
20. Whitehouse	J. Institute of Physical Medicine, Orange, New Jersey	20. ____
	K. Institute for Crippled and Disabled	
	L. Just-One-Break Committee	
	M. Mentally Retarded	
	N. Mobility Incorporated	
	O. Multiple Sclerosis	
	P. N.Y.U. Bellevue Rehabilitation	
	Q. Office of Vocational Rehabilitation	
	R. Organ Inferiority	
	S. Psychiatric Aspects	
	T. Social Psychology of Adjustment	
	U. Tuberculosis	
	V. Woodrow Wilson Rehabilitation Center	
	W. Woody	

KEY (CORRECT ANSWERS)

1.	B	11.	T	
2.	A	12.	E	
3.	D	13.	M	
4.	B	14.	J	
5.	B	15.	D	
6.	C	16.	S	
7.	D	17.	P	
8.	A	18.	I	
9.	D	19.	Q	
10.	C	20.	A	

EXAMINATION SECTION
TEST 1

DIRECTIONS: Each question or incomplete statement is followed by several suggested answers or completions. Select the one that BEST answers the question or completes the statement. *PRINT THE LETTER OF THE CORRECT ANSWER IN THE SPACE AT THE RIGHT.*

1. Studies show that handicapped persons rehabilitated under the state-federal vocational rehabilitation program repay in Federal income taxes *alone* the Federal government's ENTIRE investment in their rehabilitation within _____ year(s).   1.____

    A. one   B. three   C. six   D. ten

2. It is estimated that the number of individuals added to those who need vocational rehabilitation services each year in the United States approximates   2.____

    A. 50,000   B. 250,000   C. 1,000,000   D. 25,000,000

3. National *Employ the Physically Handicapped Week* is USUALLY observed during the month of   3.____

    A. February   B. May   C. August   D. October

4. The one of the following of the Federal aid programs of public assistance which was MOST recently developed is aid to   4.____

    A. citizens over 65 years of age not covered by social security
    B. dependent children
    C. permanently and totally disabled individuals
    D. the blind

5. The one of the following providing placement services for the physically handicapped which restricts its activities to veterans is   5.____

    A. Federation Employment Service
    B. Fifty-two Association
    C. Just-One-Break Committee
    D. Vocational Advisory Service

6. The one of the following hospitals which does NOT have a full physical medicine and rehabilitation service with a complete rehabilitation *team* is   6.____

    A. Bellevue   B. Bird S. Coler
    C. Goldwater Memorial   D. James Ewing

7. Of the following programs of services to the physically handicapped, the one which is a division of the State Department of Education is   7.____

    A. Governor's Committee on Employment of the Physically Handicapped
    B. State Rehabilitation Hospital
    C. Vocational Rehabilitation
    D. Workmen's Compensation

8. The one of the following which constitutes the LARGEST professional group in the National Rehabilitation Association is

   A. counselors
   B. occupational therapists
   C. physical therapists
   D. physicians

9. Three of the following conduct vocational training services for the handicapped. The one which does NOT is

   A. Altro Workshops
   B. American Rehabilitation Committee
   C. The Institute of Physical Medicine and Rehabilitation
   D. The Lighthouse

10. The one of the following that has a sheltered workshop IN ADDITION TO its other rehabilitation facilities is

    A. Bellevue Hospital Physical Medicine and Rehabilitation Service
    B. Hospital for Special Surgery
    C. Institute of Physical Medicine and Rehabilitation
    D. Institute for the Crippled and Disabled

11. The one of the following agencies that does NOT provide direct services to the handicapped is the

    A. American Rehabilitation Committee
    B. Federation of the Handicapped
    C. Goodwill Rehabilitation Committee
    D. International Society for the Welfare of Cripples

12. Of the following agencies, the one which is PARTICULARLY known for its program of rehabilitation for the tuberculous is the

    A. Altro Workshops
    B. Brooklyn Bureau of Social Service
    C. Federation of the Handicapped
    D. Goodwill Industries

13. Of the following agencies, the one which does NOT provide vocational counseling services for the physically handicapped is the

    A. Bureau of Social Services
    B. Federation Employment Service
    C. Fountain House
    D. Just-One-Break Committee

14. The one of the following publications which would be LEAST likely to be of professional interest to a rehabilitation counselor is

    A. COMEBACK
    B. JOURNAL OF REHABILITATION
    C. JOURNAL OF THE ASSOCIATION FOR PHYSICAL AND MENTAL REHABILITATION
    D. PERFORMANCE

15. Each municipal hospital which has a department of physical medicine and rehabilitation has a *rehabilitation team*.
    The one of the following occupations which is NOT represented on that team is

    A. bracemaker
    B. physiatrist
    C. psychologist
    D. recreation leader

16. Of the following, the one which is NOT considered to be a medical center is

    A. Beekman-Downtown
    B. Columbia-Presbyterian
    C. New York-Cornell
    D. New York University-Bellevue

17. The National Institutes of Health are a part of the

    A. Kellogg Foundation
    B. National Research Council
    C. Rockefeller Foundation
    D. U.S. Public Health Service

18. Results of I.Q. tests are used as predictors of all of the following EXCEPT

    A. learning disabilities
    B. educational achievement
    C. job performance
    D. athletic ability

19. The index usually used to describe an individual's relative mental brightness is

    A. C.A.
    B. E.Q.
    C. I.Q.
    D. M.A.

20. Of the following, the BEST criterion of an individual's normalcy is his

    A. educational goals
    B. interpersonal relationships
    C. moral values
    D. physical standards

21. The one of the following which has been greatly expanded by federal legislation is the

    A. counseling services for disabled veterans provided by the Veterans Administration
    B. federal-state vocational rehabilitation program
    C. rehabilitation training activities of the Children's Bureau
    D. selective placement activities of the various state employment services

22. The one of the following who would be LEAST likely to qualify for services under the federal-state vocational rehabilitation program is a

    A. college student paralyzed by poliomyelitis
    B. migratory worker stricken by multiple sclerosis
    C. self-employed man, fifty years of age, disabled by arthritis
    D. worker suffering from an amputation as a result of an industrial accident

23. Of the following, the present policy governing provision of medical services by the Veterans Administration to veterans with non-service connected disabilities is that

    A. if a veteran cannot afford to pay for medical care, and if a bed is available, he can receive in-patient care
    B. if a veteran cannot afford to pay for medical care, he can receive out-patient care
    C. in-patient care can be given only to those with tuberculosis
    D. out-patient care can be given only to those with psychiatric problems

24. In terms of vocational rehabilitation, the MOST important area of information which the counselor must know about the patient is his

    A. educational achievement
    B. expressed goal
    C. previous job experience
    D. type of military service discharge

25. The type of counseling MOST likely to benefit a patient who is still unable to accept his disability two years after injury has occurred is

    A. educational   B. personal   C. social   D. vocational

KEY (CORRECT ANSWERS)

1. B		11. D	
2. B		12. A	
3. D		13. C	
4. C		14. C	
5. B		15. A	
6. D		16. A	
7. C		17. D	
8. A		18. D	
9. C		19. C	
10. D		20. B	

21. B
22. B
23. A
24. B
25. B

TEST 2

DIRECTIONS: Each question or incomplete statement is followed by several suggested answers or completions. Select the one that BEST answers the question or completes the statement. *PRINT THE LETTER OF THE CORRECT ANSWER IN THE SPACE AT THE RIGHT.*

1. The development of objective criteria for measuring the physical capacities of patients is MOST difficult in cases of

    A. coronary heart disease
    B. multiple sclerosis
    C. poliomyelitis
    D. rheumatoid arthritis

    1.____

2. The prognosis for vocational rehabilitation is LEAST favorable in cases of

    A. amputation of both upper extremities
    B. diabetes
    C. hemiplegia
    D. muscular dystrophy

    2.____

3. The term used for a medical specialist in *physical medicine and rehabilitation* is

    A. orthopedist
    B. physiatrist
    C. physical therapist
    D. physiotherapist

    3.____

4. It is *generally* accepted that the sense through which people learn MOST readily is the

    A. auditory   B. kinesthetic   C. tactile   D. visual

    4.____

5. An obturator is FREQUENTLY used with persons afflicted with

    A. aphasia
    B. cleft palate
    C. lisping
    D. stuttering

    5.____

6. Visual acuity of *20/200 or less* is USUALLY interpreted as

    A. ability to discriminate between light and dark
    B. complete blindness
    C. remediable with glasses
    D. industrial blindness

    6.____

7. Of the following, the BEST means for testing hearing ability is the

    A. audiometer
    B. hearing aid
    C. medical examination of the ear
    D. watch tick test

    7.____

8. Recent studies indicate that adults suffering from a hearing loss, when compared to those with normal hearing, are *usually* MORE

    A. aggressive   B. intelligent   C. shy   D. stable

    8.____

9. The perception of one's own muscular movement is called

    A. cataplasia
    B. kinesthesia
    C. synesthesia
    D. none of the above

    9.____

10. The one of the following types of speech disorders which will *usually* respond to therapy and retraining in the SHORTEST time is

    A. articulatory disorders
    B. cleft palate speech
    C. post-laryngectomy speech
    D. stuttering

11. As a result of medical care advances, there has been, within recent years, a lessening of the need for rehabilitation counseling services in hospitals for patients with

    A. amputations
    B. arthritis
    C. hemiplegia
    D. tuberculosis

12. The one of the following conditions which is NOT characterized by an orthopedic involvement is

    A. amputations
    B. congenital club foot
    C. diabetes
    D. scoliosis

13. The use of isonicotinic hydrazides in connection with other forms of therapy is a RECENT development in the treatment of

    A. arthritis
    B. cerebral palsy
    C. muscular dystrophy
    D. tuberculosis

14. The one of the following diseases in which insulin is used as a method of medical control and management is

    A. diabetes
    B. epilepsy
    C. rheumatic fever
    D. syphilis

15. The one of the following with which aphasia is MOST commonly associated is

    A. hemiplegia   B. monoplegia   C. paraplegia   D. quadraplegia

16. The kind of patient with which a rehabilitation counselor in a municipal hospital would come into professional contact LEAST frequently is the

    A. geriatric   B. neurologic   C. orthopedic   D. psychiatric

17. In the development of the embryo, the month after which the central nervous system, origin of overt human behavior, is well under way is the

    A. second   B. fifth   C. seventh   D. ninth

18. Three of the following symptoms are frequently associated with multiple sclerosis. The one which is NOT is

    A. metabolic disturbances
    B. speech difficulties
    C. stumbling gait
    D. visual disturbances

19. Of the following, the term which does NOT describe a type of cerebral palsy is

    A. amebiasis   B. ataxic   C. athetoid   D. spastic

20. Three of the following diseases are frequently progressive in the chronic stages. The one which is NOT is

    A. multiple sclerosis
    B. muscular dystrophy
    C. Parkinson's disease
    D. poliomyelitis

21. Three of the following are diseases usually classified as chronic neurological diseases. The one which does NOT fall into this category is

   A. cerebral palsy
   B. multiple sclerosis
   C. muscular dystrophy
   D. rheumatism

22. The one of the following books that should be of MOST interest to the cerebral palsied is

   A. BORN THAT WAY by Earl R. Carlson
   B. IT WAS NOT MY OWN IDEA by Robinson Pierce
   C. TRIUMPH CLEAR by Lorraine L. Beim
   D. WHO WALK ALONE by Perry Burgess

23. In general, the percentage of patients stricken with poliomyelitis who will be severely disabled is *approximately*

   A. 20%   B. 45%   C. 75%   D. 90%

24. With the development of anticonvulsant drugs, the percentage of persons with epilepsy whose seizures can now be completely controlled is *approximately*

   A. 10%   B. 33%   C. 50%   D. 75%

25. The one of the following diseases which affects the SMALLEST number of persons is

   A. arteriosclerosis
   B. congenital heart disease
   C. hypertension
   D. rheumatic fever

26. Recent advances in the research and treatment of epilepsy have resulted from the development and widespread use of the

   A. electrocardiograph
   B. electroencephalograph
   C. electromyograph
   D. electronic microscope

27. The one of the following books that should be MOST interesting to parents of a congenital amputee is

   A. AND NOW TO LIVE AGAIN by Betsy Barton
   B. OUT ON A LIMB by Louise Baker
   C. THE CHILD WHO NEVER GREW by Pearl Buck
   D. TRIUMPH OF LOVE by Leona Bruckner

28. The one of the following responsible for the GREATEST number of patients in mental hospitals is

   A. drug addiction
   B. paresis
   C. schizophrenia
   D. senile dementia

29. Of the following, the LEAST important factor in counseling a patient with a unilateral BK amputation is

   A. diagnosis
   B. etiology
   C. site of amputation
   D. type of prosthetic device worn

30. One of the MOST comprehensive references on the psychological aspects of the physically disabled is that compiled by 30.____
    A. Bitner   B. Garrett   C. Kessler   D. Zohl

KEY (CORRECT ANSWERS)

1.	A	16.	D
2.	D	17.	A
3.	B	18.	A
4.	D	19.	A
5.	B	20.	D
6.	D	21.	D
7.	A	22.	A
8.	C	23.	A
9.	B	24.	C
10.	A	25.	B
11.	D	26.	B
12.	C	27.	D
13.	D	28.	C
14.	A	29.	D
15.	A	30.	B

EXAMINATION SECTION
TEST 1

DIRECTIONS: Each question or incomplete statement is followed by several suggested answers or completions. Select the one that BEST answers the question or completes the statement. *PRINT THE LETTER OF IN THE CORRECT ANSWER THE SPACE AT THE RIGHT.*

1. Reports show that more men than women are physically handicapped MAINLY because

    A. women are instinctively more cautious than men
    B. men are more likely to have congenital deformities
    C. women tend to seek surgical remedies because of greater concern over personal appearance
    D. men have lower ability to recover from injury
    E. men are more likely to be exposed to hazardous conditions

1._____

2. Of the following, the explanation married women give MOST frequently for seeking employment outside the home is that they wish to

    A. escape the drudgeries of home life
    B. develop secondary employment skills
    C. maintain an emotionally satisfying career
    D. provide the main support for the family
    E. supplement the family income

2._____

3. Of the following home conditions, the one *most likely* to cause emotional disturbances in children is

    A. increased birthrate following the war
    B. disrupted family relationships
    C. lower family income than that of neighbors
    D. higher family income than that of neighbors
    E. overcrowded living conditions

3._____

4. Casual unemployment, as distinguished from other types of unemployment, is traceable MOST readily to

    A. a decrease in the demand for labor as a result of scientific progress
    B. more or less haphazard changes in the demand for labor in certain industries
    C. periodic changes in the demand for labor in certain industries
    D. disturbances and disruptions in industry resulting from international trade barriers
    E. increased mobility of the population

4._____

5. Labor legislation, although primarily intended for the benefit of the employee, MAY aid the employer by

    A. increasing his control over the immediate labor market
    B. prohibiting government interference with operating policies
    C. protecting him, through equalization of labor costs, from being undercut by other employers
    D. transferring to the general taxpayer the principal costs of industrial hazards of accident and unemployment
    E. increasing the pensions of civil service employees

5._____

6. When employment and unemployment figures both decline, the MOST probable conclusion is that

    A. the population has reached a condition of equilibrium
    B. seasonal employment has ended
    C. the labor force has decreased
    D. payments for unemployment insurance have been increased
    E. industrial progress has reduced working hours

7. An individual with an I.Q. of 100 may be said to have demonstrated _____ intelligence.

    A. superior
    B. absolute
    C. substandard
    D. approximately average
    E. high average

8. While state legislatures differ in many respects, all of them are *most nearly* alike in

    A. provisions for retirement of members
    B. rate of pay
    C. length of legislative sessions
    D. method of selection of their members
    E. length of term of office

9. If a state passed a law in a field under Congressional jurisdiction and if Congress subsequently passed contrary legislation, the state provision would be

    A. regarded as never having existed
    B. valid until the next session of the state legislature, which would be obliged to repeal it
    C. superseded by the federal statute
    D. ratified by Congress
    E. still operative in the state involved

10. Power to pardon offenses committed against the people of the United States is vested in the

    A. Supreme Court of the United States
    B. United States District Courts
    C. Federal Bureau of Investigation
    D. United States Parole Board
    E. President of the United States

11. As distinguished from formal social control of an individual's behavior, an example of informal social control is that exerted by

    A. public opinion
    B. religious doctrine
    C. educational institutions
    D. statutes
    E. public health measures

12. The PRINCIPAL function of the jury in a jury trial is to decide questions of

    A. equity
    B. fact
    C. injunction
    D. contract
    E. law

13. Of the following rights of an individual, the one which usually depends on citizenship as distinguished from those given anyone living under the laws of the United States is the right to

    A. receive public assistance
    B. hold an elective office
    C. petition the government for redress of grievances
    D. receive equal protection of the laws
    E. be accorded a trial by jury

14. If the characteristics of a person were being studied by competent observers, it would be expected that their observations would differ MOST markedly with respect to their evaluation of the person's

    A. intelligence
    B. nutritional condition
    C. temperamental characteristics
    D. weight
    E. height

15. If there are evidences of dietary deficiency in families where cereals make up a major portion of the diet, the *most likely* reason for this deficiency is that

    A. cereals cause absorption of excessive quantities of water
    B. persons who concentrate their diet on cereals do not chew their food properly
    C. carbohydrates are deleterious
    D. other essential food elements are omitted
    E. children eat cereals too rapidly

16. Although malnutrition is generally associated with poverty, dietary studies of population groups in the United States reveal that

    A. malnutrition is most often due to a deficiency of nutrients found chiefly in high-cost foods
    B. there has been overemphasis of the casual relationship between poverty and malnutrition
    C. malnutrition is found among people with sufficient money to be well fed
    D. a majority of the population in all income groups is undernourished
    E. malnutrition is not a factor in the incidence of rickets

17. The organization which has as one of its primary functions the mitigation of suffering caused by famine, fire, floods, and other national calamities is the

    A. National Safety Council
    B. Salvation Army
    C. Public Administration Service
    D. American National Red Cross
    E. American Legion

18. The MAIN difference between public welfare and private social agencies is that in public agencies,

    A. case records are open to the public
    B. the granting of assistance cannot be sufficiently flexible to meet the varying needs of individual recipients
    C. only financial assistance may be provided
    D. all policies and procedures must be based upon statutory authorizations
    E. economical and efficient administration are stressed because their funds are obtained through public taxation

19. A recipient of relief who is in need of the services of an attorney but is unable to pay the customary fees, should *generally* be referred to the

    A. Small Claims Court
    B. Domestic Relations Court
    C. County Lawyers Association
    D. City Law Department
    E. Legal Aid Society

20. An injured workman should file his claim for workmen's compensation with the

    A. State Labor Relations Board
    B. Division of Placement and Unemployment Insurance
    C. State Industrial Commission
    D. Workmen's Compensation Board
    E. State Insurance Board

21. The type of insurance found MOST frequently among families such as those assisted by the Department of Social Services is

    A. accident
    B. straight life
    C. endowment
    D. industrial
    E. personal liability

22. Of the following items in the standard budget of the Department of Social Services, the one for which actual expenditures would be MOST constant throughout the year is

    A. fuel
    B. housing
    C. medical care
    D. clothing
    E. household replacements

23. The MOST frequent cause of "broken homes" is attributed to the

    A. temperamental incompatibilities of parents and in-laws
    B. extension of the system of children's courts
    C. psychopathic irresponsibility of the parents
    D. institutionalization of one of the spouses
    E. death of one or both spouses

24. In rearing children, the problems of the widower are usually greater than those of the widow, largely because of the

    A. tendency of widowers to impose excessively rigid moral standards
    B. increased economic hardship
    C. added difficulty of maintaining a desirable home
    D. possibility that a stepmother will be added to the household
    E. prevalent masculine prejudice against pursuits which are inherently feminine

24.____

25. Foster-home placement of children is often advocated in preference to institutionalization *primarily* because

    A. the law does not provide for local supervision of children's institutions
    B. institutions furnish a more expensive type of care
    C. the number of institutions is insufficient compared to the number of children needing care
    D. children are not well treated in institutions
    E. foster homes provide a more normal environment for children

25.____

KEY (CORRECT ANSWERS)

1.	E		11.	A
2.	E		12.	B
3.	B		13.	B
4.	B		14.	C
5.	C		15.	D
6.	C		16.	C
7.	D		17.	D
8.	D		18.	D
9.	C		19.	E
10.	E		20.	D

21. D
22. B
23. E
24. C
25. E

TEST 2

DIRECTIONS: Each question or incomplete statement is followed by several suggested answers or completions. Select the one that BEST answers the question or completes the statement. *PRINT THE LETTER OF THE CORRECT ANSWER IN THE SPACE AT THE RIGHT.*

1. Of the following, the category MOST likely to yield the greatest reduction in cost to the taxpayer under improved employment conditions is

    A. home relief, including aid to the homeless
    B. aid to the blind
    C. aid to dependent children
    D. old-age assistance

2. One of the MOST common characteristics of the chronic alcoholic is

    A. low intelligence level
    B. wanderlust
    C. psychosis
    D. egocentricity

3. Of the following factors leading toward the cure of the alcoholic, the MOST important is thought to be

    A. removal of all alcohol from the immediate environment
    B. development of a sense of personal adequacy
    C. social disapproval of drinking
    D. segregation from former companions

4. The Federal Housing Administration is the agency which

    A. insures mortgages made by lending institutions for new construction or remodeling of old construction
    B. provides federal aid for state and local government for slum clearance and housing for very low income families
    C. subsidizes the building industry through direct grants
    D. provides for the construction of low-cost housing projects owned and operated by the federal government

5. In comparing the advantages of foster home over institutional placement, it is generally agreed that institutional care is LEAST advisable for children

    A. who cannot sustain the intimacy of foster family living because of their experiences with their own parents
    B. who are socially well-adjusted or have had considerable experience in living with a family
    C. who have need for special facilities for observation, diagnosis, and treatment
    D. whose natural parents find it difficult to accept the idea of foster home placement because of its close resemblance to adoption

6. The school can play a vital part in detecting the child who displays overt symptomatic behavior indicative of social maladjustment CHIEFLY because the teacher has the opportunity to

    A. assume a pseudo-parental role in regard to discipline and punishment, thereby limiting the extent of the maladjusted child's anti-social behavior
    B. observe how the child relates to the group and what reactions are stimulated in him by his peer relationships
    C. determine whether the adjustment difficulties displayed by the child were brought on by the teacher herself or by the other students
    D. help the child's parents to resolve the difficulties in adjustment which are indicated by the child's reactions to the social pressures exerted by his peers

7. In treating juvenile delinquents, it has been found that there are some who make better social adjustment through group treatment than through an individual casework approach.
   In selecting delinquent boys for group treatment, the one of the following which is the MOST important consideration is that

    A. the boys to be treated in one group be friends or from the same community
    B. only boys who consent to group treatment be included in the group
    C. the ages of the boys included in the group vary as much as possible
    D. only boys who have not reacted to an individual casework approach be included in the group

8. Multi-problem families are generally characterized by various functional indicators.
   Of the following, the family which is *most likely* to be a multi-problem family is one which has

    A. unemployed adult family members
    B. parents with diagnosed character disorders
    C. children and parents with a series of difficulties in the community
    D. poor housekeeping standards

9. Multi-problem families generally have a complex history of intervention by a variety of social agencies.
   Of the following phases involved in planning for their treatment, the one which is MOST important to consider FIRST is the

    A. joint decision to limit any help to be given
    B. analysis of facts and definition of the problems involved
    C. determination of treatment priorities
    D. study of available community resources

10. The development of good public relations in the area for which the supervisor is responsible should be considered by the supervisor as

    A. not his responsibility as he is primarily responsible for his workers' services
    B. dependent upon him as he is in the best position to interpret the department to the community
    C. not important to the adequate functioning of the department
    D. a part of his method of carrying out his job responsibility as what his workers do affects the community

11. Of the following, the LEAST accurate statement concerning the relationship of public and private social agencies is that

    A. both have an important and necessary function to perform
    B. they are not to be considered as competing or rival agencies
    C. they are cooperating agencies
    D. their work is based on fundamentally different social work concepts

12. Of the following, the LEAST accurate statement concerning the worker-client relationship is that the worker should have the ability to

    A. express warmth of feeling in appropriate ways as a basis for a professional relationship which creates confidence
    B. feel appropriately in the relationship without losing the ability to see the situation in the perspective necessary to help the people immersed in it
    C. identify himself with the client so that the worker's personality does not influence the client
    D. use keen observation and perceive what is significant with a new range of appreciation of the meaning of the situation to the client

13. Of the following, the MOST fundamental psychological concept underlying case work in the public assistance field is that

    A. eligibility for public assistance should be reviewed from time to time
    B. workers should be aware of the prevalence of psychological disabilities among members of families on public assistance
    C. workers should realize the necessity of carrying out the policies laid down by the state office in order that state aid may be received
    D. in the process of receiving assistance, recipients should not be deprived of their normal status of self-direction

14. Of the following, the MOST comprehensive as well as the MOST accurate statement concerning the professional attitude of the social worker is that he should

    A. have a real concern for, and an intelligent interest in, the welfare of the client
    B. recognize that the client's feelings rather than the realities of his needs are of major importance to the client
    C. put at the client's service the worker's knowledge and sincere interest in him
    D. use his insight and understanding to make sound decisions about the client

15. The one of the following reasons for refusing a job which is LEAST acceptable, from the viewpoint of maintaining a client's continued rights to unemployment insurance benefits, is that

    A. acceptance of the job would interfere with the client's joining or retaining membership in a labor union
    B. there is a strike, lockout, or other industrial controversy in the establishment where employment is offered
    C. the distance from the place of employment to his home is greater than seems justified to the client
    D. the wages offered are lower than the prevailing wages in that locality

16. Experience pragmatically suggests that dislocation from cultural roots and customs makes for tension, insecurity, and anxiety. This holds for the child as well as the adolescent, for the new immigrant as well as the second-generation citizen.
    Of the following, the MOST important implication of the above statement for a social worker in any setting is that

    A. anxiety, distress, and incapacity are always personal and can be understood best only through an understanding of the child's present cultural environment
    B. in order to resolve the conflicts caused by the displacement of a child from a home with one cultural background to one with another, it is essential that the child fully replace his old culture with the new one
    C. no treatment goal can be envisaged for a dislocated child which does not involve a value judgment which is itself culturally determined
    D. anxiety and distress result from a child's reaction to culturally oriented treatment goals

17. Accepting the fact that mentally gifted children represent superior heredity, the United States faces an important eugenic problem CHIEFLY because

    A. unless these mentally gifted children mature and reproduce more rapidly than the less intelligent children, the nation is heading for a lowering of the average intelligence of its people
    B. although the mentally gifted child always excels scholastically, he generally has less physical stamina than the normal child and tends to lower the nation's population physically
    C. the mentally subnormal are increasing more rapidly than the mentally gifted in America, thus affecting the overall level of achievement of the gifted child
    D. unless the mental level of the general population is raised to that of the gifted child, the mentally gifted will eventually usurp the reigns of government and dominate the mentally weaker

18. The form of psychiatric treatment which requires the LEAST amount of participation on the part of the patient is

    A. psychoanalysis
    B. psychotherapy
    C. shock therapy
    D. non-directive therapy

19. Tests administered by psychologists for the PRIMARY purpose of measuring intelligence are known as _____ tests.

    A. projective
    B. validating
    C. psychometric
    D. apperception

20. In recent years, there have been some significant changes in the treatment of patients in state psychiatric hospitals. These changes are PRIMARILY caused by the use of

    A. electric shock therapy
    B. tranquilizing drugs
    C. steroids
    D. the open-ward policy

21. The psychological test which makes use of a set of twenty pictures, each depicting a dramatic scene, is known as the

    A. Goodenough Test
    B. Thematic Apperception Test
    C. Minnesota Multiphasic Personality Inventory
    D. Healy Picture Completion Test

22. One of the MOST effective ways in which experimental psychologists have been able to study the effects on personality of heredity and environment has been through the study of

    A. primitive cultures
    B. identical twins
    C. mental defectives
    D. newborn infants

23. In hospitals with psychiatric divisions, the psychiatric function is PREDOMINANTLY that of

    A. the training of personnel in all psychiatric disciplines
    B. protection of the community against potentially dangerous psychiatric patients
    C. research and study of psychiatric patients so that new knowledge and information can be made generally available
    D. short-term hospitalization designed to determine diagnosis and recommendations for treatment

24. Predictions of human behavior on the basis of past behavior frequently are INACCURATE because

    A. basic patterns of human behavior are in a continual state of flux
    B. human behavior is not susceptible to explanation of a scientific nature
    C. the underlying psychological mechanisms of behavior are not completely understood
    D. quantitative techniques for the measurement of stimuli and responses are unavailable

25. Socio-cultural factors are being re-evaluated in casework practice as they influence both the worker and the client in their participation in the casework process.
Of the following factors, the one which is currently being studied MOST widely is the

   A. social class of worker and client and its significance in casework
   B. difference in native intelligence which can be ascribed to racial origin of an individual
   C. cultural values affecting the areas in which an individual functions
   D. necessity in casework treatment of the client's membership in an organized religious group

---

KEY (CORRECT ANSWERS)

1. A
2. D
3. B
4. A
5. B

6. B
7. B
8. C
9. B
10. D

11. D
12. C
13. D
14. C
15. C

16. C
17. A
18. C
19. C
20. B

21. B
22. B
23. D
24. C
25. C

EXAMINATION SECTION
TEST 1

DIRECTIONS: Each question or incomplete statement is followed by several suggested answers or completions. Select the one that BEST answers the question or completes the statement. *PRINT THE LETTER OF THE CORRECT ANSWER IN THE SPACE AT THE RIGHT.*

1. Deviant behavior is a sociological term used to describe behavior which is not in accord with generally accepted standards. This may include juvenile delinquency, adult criminality, mental or physical illness.
   Comparison of normal with deviant behavior is useful to social workers because it

   A. makes it possible to establish watertight behavioral descriptions
   B. provides evidence of differential social behavior which distinguishes deviant from normal behavior
   C. indicates that deviant behavior is of no concern to social workers
   D. provides no evidence that social role is a determinant of behavior

   1.____

2. Alcoholism may affect an individual client's ability to function as a spouse, parent, worker, and citizen.
   A social worker's MAIN responsibility to a client with a history of alcoholism is to

   A. interpret to the client the causes of alcoholism as a disease syndrome
   B. work with the alcoholic's family to accept him as he is and stop trying to reform him
   C. encourage the family of the alcoholic to accept casework treatment
   D. determine the origins of his particular drinking problem, establish a diagnosis, and work out a treatment plan for him

   2.____

3. There is a trend to regard narcotic addiction as a form of illness for which the current methods of intervention have not been effective.
   Research on the combination of social, psychological, and physical causes of addiction would indicate that social workers should

   A. oppose hospitalization of addicts in institutions
   B. encourage the addict to live normally at home
   C. recognize that there is no successful treatment for addiction and act accordingly
   D. use the existing community facilities differentially for each addict

   3.____

4. A study of social relationships among delinquent and non-delinquent youth has shown that

   A. delinquent youth generally conceal their true feelings and maintain furtive social contacts
   B. delinquents are more impulsive and vivacious than law-abiding boys
   C. non-delinquent youths diminish their active social relationships in order to sublimate any anti-social impulses
   D. delinquent and non-delinquent youths exhibit similar characteristics of impulsiveness and vivaciousness

   4.____

5. The one of the following which is the CHIEF danger of interpreting the delinquent behavior of a child in terms of morality *alone* when attempting to get at its causes is that

    A. this tends to overlook the likelihood that the causes of the child's actions are more than a negation of morality and involve varied symptoms of disturbance
    B. a child's moral outlook toward life and society is largely colored by that of his parents, thus encouraging parent-child conflict
    C. too careful a consideration of the moral aspects of the offense and of the child's needs may often negate the demands of justice in a case
    D. standards of morality may be of no concern to the delinquent and he may not realize the seriousness of his offenses

6. Experts in the field of personnel administration are generally agreed that an employee should not be under the immediate supervision of more than one supervisor. A certain worker, because of an emergency situation, divides his time equally between two limited caseloads on a prearranged time schedule. Each unit has a different supervisor, and the worker performs substantially the same duties in each caseload.
The above statement is pertinent in this situation CHIEFLY because

    A. each supervisor, feeling that the cases in her unit should have priority, may demand too much of the worker's time
    B. the two supervisors may have different standards of work performance and may prefer different methods of doing the work
    C. the worker works part-time on each caseload and may not have full knowledge or control of the situation in either caseload
    D. the task of evaluating the worker's services will be doubled, with two supervisors instead of one having to rate his work

7. Experts in modern personnel management generally agree that employees on all job levels should be permitted to offer suggestions for improving work methods.
Of the following, the CHIEF limitation of such suggestions is that they may, at times,

    A. be offered primarily for financial reward and not show genuine interest in improvement of work methods
    B. be directed towards making individual jobs easier
    C. be restricted by the employees' fear of radically changing the work methods favored by their supervisors
    D. show little awareness of the effects on the overall objectives and functions of the entire agency

8. Through the supervisory process and relationship, the supervisor is trying to help workers gain increased self-awareness.
Of the following statements concerning this process, the one which is MOST accurate is:

    A. Self-awareness is developed gradually so that worker can learn to control his own reactions.
    B. Worker is expected to be introspective primarily for his own enlightenment.
    C. Supervisor is trying to help worker handle any emotional difficulties he may reveal.
    D. Worker is expected at the onset to share and determine with the supervisor what in his previous background makes it difficult for him to use certain ideas.

9. The one of the following statements concerning principles in the learning process which is LEAST accurate is:

   A. Some degree of regression on the part of the worker is usually natural in the process of development and this should be accepted by the supervisor.
   B. When a beginning worker shows problems, the supervisor should first handle this behavior as a personality difficulty.
   C. It has been found in the work training process that some degree of resistance is usually inevitable.
   D. The emotional content of work practice may tend to set up *blind spots* in workers.

10. Of the following, the one that represents the BEST basis for planning the content of a successful staff development program is the

   A. time available for meetings
   B. chief social problems of the community
   C. common needs of the staff workers as related to the situations with which they are dealing
   D. experimental programs conducted by other agencies

11. In planning staff development seminars, the MOST valuable topics for discussion are likely to be those selected from

   A. staff suggestions based on the staff's interest and needs
   B. topics recommended for consideration by professional organizations
   C. topics selected by the administration based on demonstrated limitations of staff skill and knowledge
   D. topics selected by the administration based on a combination of staff interest and objectivity evaluated staff needs

12. Staff meetings designed to promote professional staff development are MOST likely to achieve this goal when

   A. there is the widest participation among all staff members who attend the meetings
   B. participation by the most skilled and experienced staff members is predominant
   C. participation by selected staff members is planned before the meeting sessions
   D. supervisory personnel take major responsibility for participation

13. Assume that you are the leader of a conference attended by representatives of various city and private agencies. After the conference has been underway for a considerable time, you realize that the representative of one of these agencies has said nothing.
    It would generally be BEST for you to

   A. ask him if he would like to say anything
   B. ask the group a pertinent question that he would probably be best able to answer
   C. make no special effort to include him in the conversation
   D. address the next question you planned to ask to him directly

14. A member of a decision-making conference generally makes his BEST contribution to the conference when he

   A. compromises on his own point of view and accepts most of the points of other conference members
   B. persuades the conference to accept all or most of his points

C. persuades the conference to accept his major proposals but will yield on the minor ones
D. succeeds in integrating his ideas with the ideas of the other conference members

15. Of the following, the LEAST accurate statement concerning the compilation and use of statistics in administration is:

    A. Interpretation of statistics is as necessary as their compilation.
    B. Statistical records of expenditures and services are one of the bases for budget preparation.
    C. Statistics on the quality of services rendered to the community will clearly delineate the human values achieved.
    D. The results achieved from collecting and compiling statistics must be in keeping with the cost and effort required.

16. An important administrative problem is how precisely to define the limits on authority that is delegated to subordinate supervisors.
    Such definition of limits of authority SHOULD be

    A. as precise as possible and practicable in all areas
    B. as precise as possible and practicable in all areas of function, but should allow considerable flexibility in the area of personnel management
    C. as precise as possible and practicable in the area of personnel management, but should allow considerable flexibility in the areas of function
    D. in general terms so as to allow considerable flexibility both in the areas of function and in the areas of personnel management

17. The LEAST important of the following reasons why a particular activity should be assigned to a unit which performs activities dissimilar to it is that

    A. close coordination is needed between the particular activity and other activities performed by the unit
    B. it will enhance the reputation and prestige of the unit supervisor
    C. the unit makes frequent use of the results of this particular activity
    D. the unit supervisor has a sound knowledge and understanding of the particular activity

18. The MOST important of the following reasons why the average resident of a deteriorated slum neighborhood resists relocation to an area in the suburbs with better physical accommodations is that he

    A. does not recognize as undesirable the characteristics which are responsible for deterioration of the neighborhood
    B. has some expectation of neighborly assistance in his old home in times of stress and adversity
    C. hopes for better days when he may be able to become a figure of some importance and envy in the old neighborhood
    D. is attuned to the noise of the city and fears the quiet of the suburb

19. From a psychological and sociological point of view, the MOST important of the following dangers to the persons living in an economically depressed area in which the only step taken by governmental and private social agencies to assist these persons is the granting of a dole is that

    A. industry will be reluctant to expand its operations in that area
    B. the dole will encourage additional non-producers to enter the area
    C. the residents of the area will probably have to find their own solution to their problems
    D. their permanent dependency will be fostered

19.____

20. The term *real wages* is GENERALLY used by economists to mean the

    A. amount of take-home pay left after taxes, social security, and other such deductions have been made by the employer
    B. average wage actually earned during a calendar or fiscal year
    C. family income expressed on a per capita basis
    D. wages expressed in terms of its buyer power

20.____

21. It has, at times, been suggested that an effective way to eradicate juvenile delinquency would be to arrest and punish the parents for the criminal actions of their delinquent children.
    The one of the following which is the CHIEF defect of this proposal is that

    A. it fails to get at the cause of the delinquent act and tends to further weaken disturbed parent-child relationships
    B. since the criminally inclined child has apparently demonstrated little love or affection for his parent, the child will be unlikely to amend his behavior in order to avoid hurting his parent
    C. the child who commits anti-social acts does so in many cases in order to hurt his parents so that this proposal would not only increase the parents' sorrow, but would also serve as an incentive to more delinquency by the child
    D. the punishment should be limited to the person who commits the illegal action rather than to those who are most interested in his welfare

21.____

22. Surveys which have compared the relative stability of marriages between white persons with marriages between non-white persons in this country have shown that, among Blacks, there is

    A. a significantly higher percentage of spouses absent from the household than among whites
    B. a significantly higher percentage of spouses absent from the household than among whites living in the South, but the opposite is true in the Northeast
    C. a significantly lower percentage of spouses absent from the household than among whites
    D. no significant difference in the percentage of spouses absent from the household when compared with the white population

22.____

23. A phenomenon found in the cultural and recreational patterns of European immigrant families in America is that, generally, the foreign-born adults

    A. as well as their children, tend soon to forget their old-world activities and adopt the cultural and recreational customs of America
    B. as well as their children, tend to retain and continue their old-world cultural and recreational pursuits, and find it equally difficult to adopt those of America
    C. tend soon to drop their old pursuits and adopt the cultural and recreational patterns of America while their children find it somewhat more difficult to make this change
    D. tend to retain and continue their old-world cultural and recreational pursuits while their children tend to rapidly replace these by the games and cultural patterns of America

24. Certain mores of migrant groups are strengthened under the impact of their contact with the native society while other mores are weakened.
    In the case of Puerto Ricans who have come to the city, the effect of such contact upon their traditional family structure has been a

    A. strengthening of the former maternalistic family structure
    B. strengthening of the former paternalistic family structure
    C. weakening of the former maternalistic family structure
    D. weakening of the former paternalistic family structure

25. Administrative reviews and special studies of independent experts, as reported by the Department of Health, Education and Welfare, indicate that the proportion of recipients of public assistance who receive such assistance through *wilful misrepresentation* of the facts is

    A. less than 1%   B. about 4%
    C. between 4% and 7%   D. between 7% and 10%

KEY (CORRECT ANSWERS)

1.	B	11.	D
2.	D	12.	A
3.	D	13.	B
4.	B	14.	D
5.	A	15.	C
6.	B	16.	A
7.	D	17.	B
8.	A	18.	B
9.	B	19.	D
10.	C	20.	D

21. A
22. A
23. D
24. D
25. A

TEST 2

DIRECTIONS: Each question or incomplete statement is followed by several suggested answers or completions. Select the one that BEST answers the question or completes the statement. *PRINT THE LETTER OF THE CORRECT ANSWER IN THE SPACE AT THE RIGHT.*

1. In order to meet more adequately the public assistance needs occasioned by sudden changes in the national economy, social service agencies, in general, recommend, as a matter of preference, that

    A. each locality build up reserve funds to care for needy unemployed persons in order to avoid a breakdown of local resources such as occurred during the depression
    B. the federal government assume total responsibility for the administration of public assistance
    C. state settlement laws be strictly enforced so that unemployed workers will be encouraged to move from the emergency industry centers to their former homes
    D. a federal-state-local program of general assistance be established with need as the only eligibility requirement
    E. eligibility requirements be tightened to assure that only legitimately worthy local residents receive the available assistance

1.____

2. The MOST practical method of maintaining income for the majority of aged persons who are no longer able to work, or for the families of those workers who are deceased, is a(n)

    A. comprehensive system of non-categorical assistance on a basis of cash payments
    B. integrated system of public assistance and extensive work relief programs
    C. co-ordinated system of providing care in institutions and foster homes
    D. system of contributory insurance in which a cash benefit is paid as a matter of right
    E. expanded system of diagnostic and treatment centers

2.____

3. With the establishment of insurance and assistance programs under the Social Security Act, many institutional programs for the aged have tended to the greatest extent toward an increased emphasis on providing, of the following types of assistance,

    A. care for the aged by denominational groups
    B. care for children requiring institutional treatment
    C. recreational facilities for the able-bodied aged
    D. training facilities in industrial homework for the aged
    E. care for the chronically ill and infirm aged

3.____

4. Of the following terms, the one which BEST describes the Social Security Act is

    A. enabling legislation
    B. regulatory statute
    C. appropriations act
    D. act of mandamus
    E. provisional enactment

4.____

2 (#2)

5. Of the following, the term which MOST accurately describes an appropriation is

   A. authority to spend
   B. itemized estimate
   C. *fund* accounting
   D. anticipated expenditure
   E. executive budget

6. When business expansion causes a demand for labor, the worker group which benefits MOST immediately is the group comprising

   A. employed workers
   B. inexperienced workers under 21 years of age
   C. experienced workers 21 to 25 years of age
   D. inexperienced older workers
   E. experienced workers over 40 years of age

7. The MOST important failure in our present system of providing social work services in local communities is the

   A. absence of adequate facilities for treating mental illness
   B. lack of coordination of available data and service in the community
   C. poor quality of the casework services provided by the public agencies
   D. limitations of the probation and parole services
   E. inadequacy of private family welfare services

8. Recent studies of the relationship between incidence of illness and the use of available treatment services among various population groups in the United States show that

   A. while lower-income families use medical services with greater frequency, total expenditures are greater among the upper-income groups
   B. although the average duration of a period of medical care increases with increasing income, the average frequency of obtaining care decreases with increasing income
   C. adequacy of medical service is inversely related to frequency of illness and size of family income
   D. families in the higher-income brackets have a heavier incidence of illness and make greater use of medical services than do those in the lower-income brackets
   E. both as to frequency and duration, the distribution of illness falls equally on all groups, but the use of medical services increases with income

9. The category of disease which most public health departments and authorities usually are NOT equipped to handle *directly* is that of

   A. chronic disease
   B. bronchial disturbances
   C. venereal disease
   D. mosquito-borne diseases
   E. incipient forms of tuberculosis

10. Recent statistical analyses of the causes of death in the United States indicate that medical science has now reached the stage where it would be preferable to increase its research toward control, among the following, PRINCIPALLY of

   A. accidents
   B. suicides
   C. communicable disease
   D. chronic disease
   E. infant mortality

11. Although the distinction between mental disease and mental deficiency is fairly definite, both these conditions USUALLY represent

   A. diseases of one part or organ of the body rather than of the whole person
   B. an inadequacy existing from birth or shortly afterwards and appearing as a simplicity of intelligence
   C. a deficiency developing later in life and characterized by distortions of attitude and belief
   D. inadequacies in meeting life situations and in conducting one's affairs
   E. somewhat transitory conditions characterized by disturbances of consciousness

12. According to studies made by reliable medical research organizations in the United States, differences among the states in proportion of physicians to population are MOST directly related to the

   A. geographic resources among the states
   B. skill of the physicians
   C. relative proportions of urban and rural people in the population of the states
   D. number of specialists in the ranks of the physicians
   E. health status of the people in the various states

13. One of the MAIN advantages of incorporating a charitable organization is that

   A. gifts or property of a corporation cannot be held in perpetuity
   B. gifts to unincorporated charitable organizations are not deductible from the taxable income
   C. incorporation gives less legal standing or *personality* than an informal partnership
   D. members of a corporation cannot be held liable for debts contracted by the organization
   E. a corporate organization cannot be sued

14. The BASIC principle underlying a social security program is that the government should provide

   A. aid to families that is not dependent on state or local participation
   B. assistance to any worthy family unable to maintain itself independently
   C. protection to individuals against some of the social risks that are inherent in an industrialized society
   D. safeguards against those factors leading to economic depression

15. The activities of state and local public welfare agencies are dependent to a large degree on the public assistance program of the federal government.
The one of the following which the federal government has NOT been successful in achieving within the local agencies is the

    A. broadening of the scope of public assistance administration
    B. expansion of the categorical programs
    C. improvement of the quality of service given to clients
    D. standardization of the administration of general assistance programs

16. Of the following statements, the one which BEST describes the federal government's position, as stated in the Social Security Act, with regard to tests of character or fitness to be administered by local or state welfare departments to prospective clients is that

    A. no tests of character are required but they are not specifically prohibited
    B. if tests of character are used, they must be uniform throughout the state
    C. tests of character are contrary to the philosophy of the federal government and are to be considered illegal
    D. no tests of character are required, and assistance to those states that use them will be withheld

17. An increase in the size of the welfare grant may increase the cost of the welfare program not only in terms of those already on the welfare rolls, but because it may result in an increase in the number of people on the rolls.
The CHIEF reason that an increase in the size of the grant may cause an increase in the number of people on the rolls is that the increased grant may

    A. induce low-salaried wage earners to apply for assistance rather than continue at their menial jobs
    B. make eligible for assistance many people whose resources are just above the previous standard
    C. induce many people to apply for assistance who hesitated to do so because of meagerness of the previous grant
    D. make relatives less willing to contribute because the welfare grant can more adequately cover their dependents' needs

18. One of the MAIN differences between the use of casework methods by a public welfare agency and by a private welfare agency is that the public welfare agency

    A. requires that the applicant be eligible for the services it offers
    B. cannot maintain a non-judgmental attitude toward its clients because of legal requirements
    C. places less emphasis on efforts to change the behavior of its clients
    D. must be more objective in its approach to the client because public funds are involved

19. All definitions of social casework include certain major assumptions.
Of the following, the one which is NOT considered a major assumption is that

    A. the individual and society are interdependent
    B. social forces influence behavior and attitudes, affording opportunity for self-development and contribution to the world in which we live
    C. reconstruction of the total personality and reorganization of the total environment are specific goals
    D. the client is a responsible participant at every step in the solution of his problems

20. In order to provide those services to problem families which will help restore them to a self-maintaining status, it is necessary to FIRST   20._____

   A. develop specific plans to meet the individual needs of the problem family
   B. reduce the size of those caseloads composed of multi-problem families
   C. remove them from their environment and provide them with the means of overcoming their dependency
   D. identify the factors causing their dependency and creating problems for them

21. Of the following, the type of service which can provide the client with the MOST enduring help is that service which   21._____

   A. provides him with material aid and relieves the stress of his personal problems
   B. assists him to do as much as he can for himself and leaves him free to make his own decisions
   C. directs his efforts towards returning to a self-maintaining status and provides him with desirable goals
   D. gives him the feeling that the agency is interested in him as an individual and stands ready to assist him with his problems

22. Psychiatric interpretation of unconscious motivations can bring childhood conflicts into the framework of adult understanding and open the way for them to be resolved, but the interpretation must come from within the client.   22._____
   This statement means MOST NEARLY that

   A. treatment is merely diagnosis in reverse
   B. explaining a client to himself will lead to the resolution of his problems
   C. the client must arrive at an understanding of his problems
   D. unresolved childhood conflicts create problems for the adult

23. A significant factor in the United States economic picture is the state of the labor market. Of the following, the MOST important development affecting the labor market has been   23._____

   A. an expansion of the national defense effort creating new plant capacity
   B. the general increase in personal income as a result of an increase in overtime pay in manufacturing industries
   C. the growth of manufacturing as a result of automation
   D. a demand for a large number of jobs resulting from new job applicants as well as from displacement of workers by automation

24. A typical characteristic of the United States population over 65 is that MOST of them   24._____

   A. are independent and capable of self-support
   B. live in their own homes but require various supportive services
   C. live in institutions for the aged
   D. require constant medical attention at home or in an institution

25. The one of the following factors which is MOST important in preventing persons 65 years of age and older from getting employment is the   25._____

   A. misconceptions by employers of skills and abilities of senior citizens
   B. lack of skill in modern industrial techniques of persons in this age group
   C. social security laws restricting employment of persons in this age group
   D. unwillingness of persons in this age group to continue supporting themselves

KEY (CORRECT ANSWERS)

1. D
2. D
3. E
4. A
5. A

6. B
7. B
8. C
9. A
10. D

11. D
12. C
13. D
14. C
15. D

16. A
17. B
18. C
19. C
20. D

21. B
22. C
23. D
24. B
25. A

———

EXAMINATION SECTION
TEST 1

DIRECTIONS: Each question or incomplete statement is followed by several suggested answers or completions. Select the one that BEST answers the question or completes the statement. *PRINT THE LETTER OF THE CORRECT ANSWER IN THE SPACE AT THE RIGHT.*

1. A fusion operation upon the spine is often undertaken to correct 1.____
 A. pelvimetry   B. paroxysm   C. epiphysistis   D. scoliosis

2. The treatment program for slipped epiphysis is MOST similar to the program for 2.____
 A. torticollis   B. Perthe's disease
 C. polydactylism   D. nephrosis

3. Which one of the following conditions is MOST likely to require special educational placement? Fracture of the 3.____
 A. ulna   B. radius   C. femur   D. scapula

4. Which one of the following persons was well-known for his popular newspaper articles on rehabilitation? 4.____
 A. Fred M. Hechinger   B. Howard A Rusk
 C. William M. Cruickshank   D. Merle E. Frampton

5. For the past 20 years, the leading cause of death in children has been 5.____
 A. rheumatic fever   B. poliomyelitis
 C. cancer   D. heart disease

6. Of the following, which one is the MOST frequent cause of long-term crippling conditions in children? 6.____
 A. Infections   B. Congenital defects
 C. Metabolic disturbances   D. Unknown causes

7. Which one of the following statements concerning rheumatic fever and heart disease is CORRECT? 7.____
 A. All children who have rheumatic fever will have heart disease.
 B. Some who have had rheumatic fever will have heart disease.
 C. No children who have had rheumatic fever will have heart disease.
 D. All children with heart disease have had rheumatic fever.

8. Of the following, which orthopedic disability gives rise to special educational placement of the LARGEST number of children? 8.____
 A. Slipped epiphysis   B. Multiple sclerosis
 C. Lordosis   D. Otitis

9. A disease in which the muscles appear to be replaced with fatty tissue is 9._____
   A. epiphysitis B. kyphosis
   C. muscular dystrophy D. Still's disease

10. Which one of the following BEST defines "a suffix of nouns denoting a 10._____
    morbid condition of growth"?
    A. oma B. itis C. osis D. omy

11. The formation of an artificial anus in the anterior abdominal wall or loin 11._____
    is known as a(n)
    A. anuria B. achondroplasia
    C. colostomy D. plastogene

12. Carpus, ethmoid, and coccyx are 12._____
    A. arteries B. bones C. enzymes D. ligaments

13. Inflammation of the intestinal tract is known as 13._____
    A. enteritis B. hepatitis
    C. glomerulonephritis D. rhinitis

14. Which one of the following conditions is CORRECTLY paired with an 14._____
    associated disability often found as a secondary defect?
    A. Cerebral palsy – hearing defect B. Chorea – visual defect
    C. Perthe's Disease – speech defect D. Torticollis – poor coordination

15. In which one of the following pairs is it MOST difficult to arrive at a 15._____
    differential diagnosis?
    A Encephalitis – meningitis B. Aphasia – brain damage
    C. Poliomyelitis – muscular dystrophy D. Hydrocephalia – microcephalia

16. Abnormal brain wave discharges are MOST characteristic of 16._____
    A. diabetes B. epilepsy
    C. herpes D. Hansen's disease

17. Polyarthritis is sometimes used as a synonym for 17._____
    A. acute rheumatic fever B. arthrochondritis
    C. multiple sclerosis D. polyneuritis

18. Pfeiffer's disease, glandular fever, and infectious mononucleosis are all 18._____
    A. the same disease
    B. non-communicable diseases
    C. characterized by a decrease in abnormal mononuclear cells
    D. the result of an intestinal virus

19. Prolongation of the blood clotting time results from a deficiency of vitamin 19._____
    A. B2 B. K C. E D. D

20. Which one of the following is classified as a fissure of the brain?   20.____
    A. Maxillary plexuses   B. Periphlebitis
    C. Visceral cleavage   D. Parieto-occipital

21. Paralysis of corresponding parts on two sides of the body is known as   21.____
    A. diplegia   B. hemiplegia   C. monoplegia   D. hemiparesis

22. Muscular dystrophy is a condition in which   22.____
    A. the cause is known
    B. there is apparently no hereditary transmission
    C. several members of the family are often affected in the same manner
    D. the juvenile type is rarely found in boys

23. Tachycardia is a condition of the _____ system.   23.____
    A. skeletal   B. endocrine   C. circulatory   D. digestive

24. Which one of the following diseases involves the lymph nodes and has a poor prognosis?   24.____
    A. Colitis   B. Ileitis
    C. Lordosis   D. Hodgkin's Disease

25. Of the following diseases, the one that is NOT directly attributable to a specific vitamin deficiency is   25.____
    A. scurvy   B. beriberi   C. tularemia   D. pellagra

KEY (CORRECT ANSWERS)

1.	D	11.	C
2.	B	12.	B
3.	C	13.	A
4.	B	14.	A
5.	D	15.	B
6.	B	16.	B
7.	B	17.	A
8.	A	18.	A
9.	C	19.	B
10.	A	20.	D

21. A
22. C
23. C
24. D
25. C

TEST 2

DIRECTIONS: Each question or incomplete statement is followed by several suggested answers or completions. Select the one that BEST answers the question or completes the statement. *PRINT THE LETTER OF THE CORRECT ANSWER IN THE SPACE AT THE RIGHT.*

1. The three bones known as the "hammer, anvil, and stirrup" are found in the human 1.____
   A. nose   B. knee   C. ear   D. elbow

2. Of the following body functions, the one performed by the white blood cells is 2.____
   A. carrying carbon dioxide to the lungs
   B. destroying invading bacteria
   C. carrying food particles to the cells
   D. destroying old red blood corpuscles

3. Of the following, the word "dyspnea" is MOST closely associated with 3.____
   A. bronchial asthma   B. meningitis
   C. rickets   D. synovitis

4. A disease characterized by tonic spasms in the voluntarily moved muscles is 4.____
   A. osteomyelitis   B. otomycosis
   C. pleuralgia   D. myotonia congenita

5. With which one of the following is the term "aura" MOST commonly associated? 5.____
   A. Psycho-motor seizures   B. Petit mal seizures
   C. Grand mal seizures   D. Laryngospasm

6. Talipes valgus and talipes varus are terms that refer to 6.____
   A. postural foot defects   B. congenital hip malformations
   C. bony protrusions   D. ailments of the bladder

7. REHABILITATION LITERATURE is a publication issued by the 7.____
   A. United States Office of Vocational Rehabilitation
   B. National Society for Crippled Children and Adults
   C. Council for Exceptional Children
   D. American Educational Research Association

8. Which one of the following physicians is MOST closely associated with work on tuberculosis of the spine? 8.____
   A. Erb   B. Bell   C. Pott   D. Friedreich

9. Which one of the following disabilities is apt to require the MOST special precautionary measures on the part of the parent and teacher? 9.____
   A. Fragilitas ossium   B. Syndactylism
   C. Rheumatic fever   D. Arthritis

10. Bursitis, spondylitis, myositis, and sciatica are diseases which are often included under the more general term
    A. thrombosis   B. rheumatism   C. arthritis   D. myxedema

11. An essential difference between nephritis and nephrosis is that nephritis
    A. is a kidney disease; nephrosis is a disease of the liver
    B. may occur at any age; nephrosis occurs only in adulthood
    C. suggests the presence of an inflammation; nephrosis occurs without signs of inflammation
    D. is relatively rare in frequency of occurrence; nephrosis occurs much more frequently

12. Which one of the following is the MAJOR defense that the body utilizes against disease-carrying germs?
    A. Red blood corpuscles   B. Riboflavin
    C. White corpuscles   D. Lymphotomes

13. Research has demonstrated that the number of epileptic seizures may be decreased through the use of psychotherapy. One may conclude from such studies that
    A. epilepsy does not involve organic brain pathology
    B. epilepsy should not be treated chemically
    C. epilepsy involves an inherent personality deformity or disorder
    D. children may react to recognizable emotional crises with hysterical convulsions

14. The wearing of braces, crutches, or casts would be apt to produce the MOST anxiety among children between the ages of
    A. 4-6   B. 7-9   C. 10-12   D. 13-15

15. According to Strauss, brain-injured retardates
    A. have a good attention span
    B. have a poorer vocabulary than the familial retardate
    C. seem to be attracted to the details of an object rather than the whole
    D. go from one task to the next with little effort

16. The transformation of anxiety into bodily symptoms similar to actual physical illness is USUALLY referred to as
    A. conversion hysteria   B. a tic
    C. a phobia   D. a compulsion

17. The following are four types of reaction of physically handicapped children to various situations:
    1) Hysteria   2) Regression
    3) Aggression   4) Attention seeking
    Which two of these reactions are MOST closely related?
    A. 1 and 4   B. 2 and 4   C. 3 and 4   D. 1 and 2

18. Large print reading materials and large charts are likely to be profitably employed for children with
    A. ataxia
    B. multiple sclerosis
    C. ileitis
    D. hemophilia

19. A child who takes a regular dosage of Dilantin is PROBABLY suffering from
    A. hepatitis   B. epilepsy   C. nephrosis   D. hypohidrosis

20. Broad spectrum antibiotics are used MAINLY for diseases caused by
    A. parasites
    B. allergens
    C. degenerative factors
    D. bacteria

21. The name "Cooley" is MOST closely associated with a form of
    A. anemia
    B. dystrophy
    C. asthma
    D. cerebral palsy

22. Chorea is a disease of the _____ system.
    A. digestive   B. respiratory   C. circulatory   D. nervous

23. "A short lapse of consciousness and a sudden momentary pause in conversation or movement" is MOST suggestive of
    A. nephrosis
    B. autism
    C. Friedreich's ataxia
    D. petit mal seizure

24. Which one of the following diseases USUALLY has a very poor prognosis?
    A. Hodgkin's Disease
    B. Slipped epiphysis
    C. Cerebral palsy
    D. Eczema

25. Mononucleosis is an abnormal condition of the
    A. blood   B. liver   C. nerves   D. colon

KEY (CORRECT ANSWERS)

1. C
2. B
3. A
4. D
5. C

6. A
7. B
8. C
9. C
10. C

11. C
12. C
13. D
14. D
15. C

16. A
17. C
18. A
19. B
20. D

21. A
22. D
23. D
24. A
25. A

TEST 3

DIRECTIONS: Each question or incomplete statement is followed by several suggested answers or completions. Select the one that BEST answers the question or completes the statement. *PRINT THE LETTER OF THE CORRECT ANSWER IN THE SPACE AT THE RIGHT.*

1. Increased thirst, increased urination, loss of weight, and general fatigue are COMMON symptoms of 1.____
    A. arthrogryposis   B. diabetes   C. hepatitis   D. arthritis

2. Dementia praecox is now COMMONLY called _____ reaction. 2.____
    A. schizophrenic   B. depressive   C. manic   D. obsessive

3. Which one of the following is a disease of the ear? 3.____
    A. Ostitis   B. Otitis   C. Omphlitis   D. Ophthalmia

4. Glomerulonephritis is a disease of the 4.____
    A. heart   B. stomach   C. kidney   D. larynx

5. Which one of the following is the disease that would MOST likely impair the ability to ambulate? 5.____
    A. Diabetes
    B. Colitis
    C. Bronchiectasis
    D. Spina bifida

6. The lay term "hunchback" is synonymous with 6.____
    A. kyphosis
    B. scoliosis
    C. torticollis
    D. spondylolisthesis

7. Which one of the following diseases involves a malformation of the heart? 7.____
    A. Hydrocele
    B. Tetralogy of Fallot
    C. Myasthenia gravis
    D. Lordosis

8. Of the following, the disease which would be included under the general classification "orthopedic" is 8.____
    A. lupus erythematosus
    B. lymphedema
    C. Osgood-Schlatter's
    D. opthalmospasm

9. Of the following cardiac classifications, the one the teacher would be LEAST likely to encounter is 9.____
    A. 4A   B. 3C   C. 4E   D. 2C

10. Which one of the following diseases is ALWAYS congenital? 10.____
    A. Cerebral palsy
    B. Osteogenesis imperfecta
    C. Rheumatoid arthritis
    D. Pericarditis

11. Of the following, which condition represents a disturbance of the neuro-muscular system frequently accompanied by perceptual difficulties? 11.____
      A. Perthe's disease   B. Cerebral palsy
      C. Spina bifida   D. Talipes

12. The following symptoms are noted in a group of children: enlargement of the calf muscles, difficulty in raising arms, afflicted shoulder and face muscles, waddling gait. The children are PROBABLY suffering from 12.____
      A. spina bifida   B. polio
      C. muscular dystrophy   D. Perthe's disease

13. Of the following diseases, which one is hereditary? 13.____
      A. Scoliosis   B. Osteomyelitis   C. Hemophilia   D. Chorea

14. In which one of the following diseases is overweight FREQUENTLY a concomitant? 14.____
      A. Pott's disease   B. Epilepsy
      C. Slipped epiphysis   D. Coxa vara

15. Hyperactivity is MOST apt to be observed in children who have 15.____
      A. muscular dystrophy   B. brain damage
      C. ileitis   D. rheumatic fever

16. Three broad categories of physical disabilities – orthopedic, cardiac and chronic – are often used for convenience in classifying children. The group below which BEST fits into the category of "chronic" is 16.____
      A. rheumatic fever, muscular dystrophy, kyphosis
      B. nephrosis, colitis, hepatitis
      C. Friedreich's ataxia, osteomyelitis, torticollis
      D. rickets, chorea, arthogryposis

17. Congenital malformation of the brain is often associated with 17.____
      A. hydrocephaly   B. myelitis
      C. varicella   D. lupus erythematosus

18. The use of an electroencephalogram usually proves MOST valuable in the diagnosis of 18.____
      A. epilepsy   B. osteoma   C. lordosis   D. nephritis

19. Incontinence is MOST often an accompanying symptom of 19.____
      A. spina bifida   B. lordosis
      C. Friedreich's ataxia   D. Hodgkin's disease

20. Which one of the following types of cerebral palsy is characterized by uncontrolled movements, facial contortions, and drooling? 20.____
      A. Ataxia   B. Spasticity   C. Athetosis   D. Rigidity

21. Which one of the following diseases may result in brain damage? 21.____
    A. Poliomyelitis   B. Lymphadenoma
    C. Spondylitis   D. Encephalitis

22. A disease USUALLY characterized by frequent vomiting and cramps is 22.____
    A. colitis   B. bronchitis   C. myocarditis   D. empyemia

23. A lateral curvature of the spine is characteristic of 23.____
    A. scoliosis   B. lordosis   C. hyphosis   D. stenosis

24. Which of the following is one of the GREAT dangers of many forms of anemia? 24.____
    A. Brain deterioration   B. Secondary infection
    C. Mental deficiency   D. Bleeding

25. A cleft of the vertebral column with meningeal protrusion is characteristic of 25.____
    A. Sprengel's deformity   B. scoliosis
    C. coxa vara   D. spina bifida

KEY (CORRECT ANSWERS)

1.	B	11.	B
2.	A	12.	C
3.	B	13.	C
4.	C	14.	C
5.	D	15.	B
6.	A	16.	B
7.	B	17.	A
8.	C	18.	A
9.	A	19.	A
10.	B	20.	C

21. D
22. A
23. A
24. B
25. D

TEST 4

DIRECTIONS: Each question or incomplete statement is followed by several suggested answers or completions. Select the one that BEST answers the question or completes the statement. *PRINT THE LETTER OF THE CORRECT ANSWER IN THE SPACE AT THE RIGHT.*

1. When correctly used, the term "allergen" refers to
   A. a person who is allergic
   B. an antihistamine medication
   C. a substance which produces allergy
   D. the tendency to inherit an allergy

2. Which of the following is congenital?
   A. Meningitis
   B. Gastro-enteritis
   C. Chronic bronchitis
   D. Osteogenesis imperfecta

3. Spasm is a common characteristic of
   A. slipped epiphysis
   B. otitis
   C. muscular dystrophy
   D. asthma

4. Which one of the following involves the degeneration of parts of the brain or spinal chord, or both?
   A. Schizophrenia
   B. Spina bifida
   C. Multiple sclerosis
   D. Pott's disease

5. Of the following, the disability with the BEST prognosis is
   A. Cooley's anemia
   B. encephalitis
   C. hemophilia
   D. slipped epiphysis

6. Infectious mononucleosis is also known as
   A. Hodgkin's disease
   B. glandular fever
   C. chorea
   D. bronchiectasis

7. Which one of the following is non-inflammatory?
   A. Cystitis   B. Nephritis   C. Nephrosis   D. Pyelitis

8. Idiopathic epilepsy may be BEST characterized as a condition which
   A. is of unknown origin
   B. is a result of some trauma
   C. is not amenable to treatment
   D. may be safely ignored

9. Which one of the following conditions is characterized by loss of weight, sleeplessness, irritability, and bulging eyes?
   A. Tuberculosis
   B. Overactive thyroid
   C. Myasthenia gravis
   D. Friedreich's ataxia

10. Cardiac involvement may result from a previous acute, infectious disease. The disease referred to is
    A. streptococcus sore throat
    B. measles
    C. uremia
    D. enteric fever

11. A type of facial paralysis due to a neuritis of the facial nerve in the Fallopian canal is called
    A. Paget's disease
    B. Bell's palsy
    C. endocarditis
    D. encephalitis

12. A slipped epiphysis occurs MOST frequently in
    A. early adolescence
    B. late adolescence
    C. pre-adolescence
    D. early childhood

13. An electroencephalogram would NOT ordinarily be used in connection with
    A. epilepsy
    B. ataxia
    C. pyelitis
    D. meningitis

14. Which of the following is characterized by lifeless muscle?
    A. Pott's disease
    B. Flaccid paralysis
    C. Scoliosis
    D. Colitis

15. The psychologist's report on a child states that he suffers from aphasia. Aphasia is a(n)
    A. impairment of the ability to use or understand spoken language
    B. disturbance of muscular coordination
    C. neurotic reaction characterized by intense fear
    D. inability consciously to recall events or personal identity

16. Which one of the following is MOST likely to be associated with production of large quantities of mucous?
    A. Kyphosis
    B. Bronchiectasis
    C. Lymphodenoma
    D. Thyroid deficiency

17. Poor bladder control is MOST frequently associated with
    A. rheumatic fever
    B. hemophilia
    C. club foot
    D. torticollis

18. Excessive accumulation of cerebrospinal fluid within the skull is USUALLY characterized as
    A. mongolism
    B. microcephaly
    C. macrocephaly
    D. hydrocephaly

19. Cerebral palsy is a term applied to a group of conditions having in common
    A. hereditary malformation
    B. retarded mentality
    C. microcephalic appearance
    D. disorders of muscular control

20. Which one of the following conditions is caused by the inflammation of the lower part of the intestine?
    A. Pyelitis
    B. Transverse myelitis
    C. Regional ileitis
    D. Hepatitis

21. In contrast with former treatment methods that called for intramuscular injections, oral medication is now frequently provided for treating
    A. diabetes   B. colitis   C. thyroiditis   D. myelitis

22. A child who has cerebral palsy has difficulty in keeping his paper on his desk. Which one of the following materials should his teacher provide to help him?
    A. A thick piece of oaktag
    B. A paperweight
    C. Masking tape
    D. A set of tacks

23. A bone fracture which is in the process of healing will call for GREATER intake of
    A. vitamin B complex
    B. folic acid
    C. vitamins D and C
    D. vitamins A and K

24. Antihistamines are often used in treating
    A. allergies
    B. anemias
    C. glandular fevers
    D. adrenal hemorrhages

25. An underweight child with a cardiac condition should be encouraged to
    A. add candy to his diet
    B. add carbohydrates such as bread and milk desserts to his diet
    C. maintain weight below normal since this ensures a margin of safety should illness occur
    D. increase his intake of fluids and salt

KEY (CORRECT ANSWERS)

1. C
2. D
3. D
4. C
5. D

6. B
7. C
8. A
9. B
10. A

11. B
12. A
13. C
14. B
15. A

16. C
17. A
18. D
19. D
20. C

21. A
22. C
23. C
24. A
25. B

TEST 5

DIRECTIONS: Each question or incomplete statement is followed by several suggested answers or completions. Select the one that BEST answers the question or completes the statement. *PRINT THE LETTER OF THE CORRECT ANSWER IN THE SPACE AT THE RIGHT.*

1. Which of the following diseases has yielded to chemotherapeutic treatment in recent years? 1.____
   A. Multiple sclerosis
   B. Tuberculosis
   C. Diabetes
   D. Scleroderma

2. The MOST satisfactory results in the treatment of epilepsy have been obtained through the use of 2.____
   A. vitamins   B. diet   C. drugs   D. exercise

3. A physically handicapped child is enclosed in a box which enables her to stand and work. The child PROBABLY suffers from 3.____
   A. scoliosis
   B. Perthe's disease
   C. spina bifida
   D. cerebral palsy

4. In which of the following are the contributing authorities CORRECTLY matched with the area of work indicated? 4.____
   A. Epilepsy – Lennox, Putnam
   B. Cardiovascular diseases – White, Cruickshank
   C. Rehabilitation – Salk, Deaver
   D. Cerebral palsy – Phelps, De La Chappelle

5. Sound vibrations are transmitted to the brain by the 5.____
   A. nerves in the inner ear
   B. nerves in the middle ear
   C. ear drum
   D. nerves of the outer ear

6. Of the following, which disease requires STRICTEST control of the time interval between meals? 6.____
   A. Rheumatic fever
   B. Allergy
   C. Diabetes
   D. Epilepsy

7. Of the following, which disease is MUCH MORE prevalent now than it was twenty years ago? 7.____
   A. Poliomyelitis
   B. Spina bifida
   C. Hemophilia
   D. Infectious hepatitis

8. Which one of the following approaches to the treatment of epilepsy has been MOST successful in recent years? 8.____
   A. Drug therapy
   B. Special diets
   C. Psychotherapy
   D. Shock therapy

9. Early research in the education of brain-injured children without motor handicaps was done by
   A. Cruickshank   B. Barker   C. Lehtinen   D. Fouracre

10. In recent years, particular attention has been paid to the educational problems presented by
   A. the brain injured
   B. hemophiliacs
   C. the orthopedically handicapped
   D. children with muscular dystrophy

11. Which one of the following may result in brain damage and mental deficiency?
   A. Meningitis and encephalitis
   B. Poliomyelitis and chorea
   C. Scarlet fever and enuresis
   D. Rheumatic fever and arthritis

12. The exact cause of rheumatic fever is unknown, but in susceptible individuals an attack is frequently proceded by
   A. respiratory streptococcal infection
   B. recurrent migraine disturbance
   C. a violent spasm of intestinal distress
   D. sustained and intense feverish disorder

13. The MOST frequent glandular condition associated with mental retardation is a deficiency in the functioning of the _____ gland.
   A. pineal   B. thyroid   C. pituitary   D. adrenal

14. Some authorities maintain that the inability of the body to utilize a vitamin properly is a causative factor in
   A. epilepsy
   B. muscular dystrophy
   C. chorea
   D. achondroplasia

15. Glandular fever is sometimes referred to as
   A. mononucleosis
   B. myasthenia gravis
   C. monoplegia
   D. ileitis

16. A metabolic disease in which there is persistent hyperglycaemia, excessive thirst, and loss of weight is
   A. cancer
   B. heart disease
   C. diabetes
   D. Addison's disease

17. Insulin, which enables the body to utilize and store sugar properly, is produced by the
   A. liver
   B. Islands of Langerhans
   C. spleen
   D. bone marrow

18. Victims of rheumatic fever are prone to develop chronic forms of
   A. dyspepsia and dysphagia
   B. sore throats and tonsillitis
   C. migraine and asthma
   D. intestinal and muscular disorder

19. A child with a positive EEG reading is likely to have 19.____
    A. asthma B. rheumatic fever
    C. convulsive disorders D. nephritis

20. Spasticity may reduce a child's ability to respond accurately to a teacher's questions requiring 20.____
    A. use of the sense of touch B. recall of prior learning
    C. knowledge of subject matter D. familiarity with domestic routines

21. Of the following, which child is MOST apt to encounter difficulty in handling spatial relationships? The child with 21.____
    A. spina bifida B. ulcerative colitis
    C. Pott's disease D. cerebral palsy

22. Which one of the following is characterized by involuntary, abnormal movements in the extremities? 22.____
    A. Myositus B. Rheumatic fever
    C. Athetosis D. Scoliosis

23. Of the following, the disease that is believed to have strong psychosomatic implications is 23.____
    A. colitis B. diabetes C. anemia D. hepatitis

24. Which one of the following is a congenital disease that involves the internal organs of the body? 24.____
    A. Cystic fibrosis B. Nephritis
    C. Tuberculosis D. Synovitis

25. Of the following disabilities, the one MOST likely to require a body cast is 25.____
    A. muscular dystrophy B. scoliosis
    C. esophagitis D. torticollis

KEY (CORRECT ANSWERS)

1.	B		11.	A
2.	C		12.	A
3.	D		13.	B
4.	A		14.	B
5.	A		15.	A
6.	C		16.	C
7.	D		17.	B
8.	A		18.	B
9.	C		19.	C
10.	A		20.	A

21. D
22. C
23. A
24. A
25. B

TEST 6

DIRECTIONS: Each question or incomplete statement is followed by several suggested answers or completions. Select the one that BEST answers the question or completes the statement. *PRINT THE LETTER OF THE CORRECT ANSWER IN THE SPACE AT THE RIGHT.*

1. Arteriosclerosis is a disturbance of the _____ system. 1.____
   A. skeletal   B. endocrine   C. nervous   D. circulatory

2. Of the following disorders, which one is NOT a form of cerebral palsy? 2.____
   A. Little's disease   B. Athetosis
   C. Mitral stenosis   D. Spastic paralysis

3. The chin is rotated away from the side of the short, prominent muscle; the head is tilted toward the affected side. These symptoms are characteristic of 3.____
   A. talipes   B. torticollis   C. ligamentitis   D. bursitis

4. A patient designated by a physician as "Class IID" is suffering from 4.____
   A. diabetes   B. polio
   C. tuberculosis   D. heart disease

5. A dorsal curvature is GENERALLY referred to as 5.____
   A. lordosis   B. hyphosis   C. scoliosis   D. curatosis

6. A disease that usually occurs in overweight boys and girls between the ages of ten and thirteen years, and is characterized by upper tibial epiphysitis is known as _____ disease. 6.____
   A. Pott's   B. Charcot-Tooth's
   C. Little's   D. Osgood-Schlatter's

7. A child whose walk is characterized by a scissors gait, with inward rotation and adduction of the legs, is PROBABLY suffering from 7.____
   A. Erb's palsy   B. spasticity
   C. osteogenesis imperfecta   D. spina bifida

8. Which one of the following groups encompasses the LARGEST number of children? 8.____
   A. Malnourished   B. Crippled   C. Cardiac   D. Tuberculosis

9. Rickets, a disease of nutrition manifested by disturbance in the general health and in the bones and joints, is caused by a lack of vitamin 9.____
   A. A   B. B   C. C   D. D

10. Rheumatic fever 10.____
    A. most often strikes children between the ages of 9 and 10
    B. is generally thought to be a streptococcal infection
    C. is generally accompanied by pain in the region of the heart
    D. is contagious

11. A young girl has to have a blood transfusion every two weeks. She PROBABLY is suffering from
    A. gastritis
    B. hepatitis
    C. nephritis
    D. Cooley's disease

12. Differential diagnosis is MOST difficult in distinguishing between cases of
    A. poliomyelitis and meningitis
    B. aphasia and brain damage
    C. spasticity and athetosis
    D. leukemia and anemia

13. In using the Snellen letter chart, an "eye test line" should be marked on the floor in the classroom _____ from the chart.
    A. 15'
    B. 20'
    C. 25'
    D. 30'

14. Adults normally have _____ teeth.
    A. 40
    B. 36
    C. 32
    D. 28

15. Of the following, the MOST important function of the sweat glands is to
    A. remove salt from the blood
    B. cool the body through evaporation
    C. cleanse the pores in the skin
    D. reduce body weight

16. Which of the following is CORRECTLY matched with the vitamin or mineral that counteracts it?
    A. Eye ailments – Vitamin K
    B. Anemia – Vitamin A
    C. Failure in blood clotting – Iron
    D. Goiter – Iodine

17. A well-balanced diet should include foods rich in minerals because they furnish the body with
    A. materials for the repair of body tissues
    B. materials for building strong teeth and bones
    C. materials for growing nails and hair
    D. energy for work

18. A physical handicap is MOST likely to be a disturbing influence to the child who is
    A. between the ages of 3 and 8
    B. between the ages of 8 and 12
    C. an adolescent
    D. a post-adolescent

19. A young aphasic child
    A. always understands what is said to him but cannot respond vocally
    B. always has a hearing loss in addition to his language disorder
    C. is usually mentally retarded
    D. shows many of the same characteristics and symptoms associated with deafness

20. The proportion of children with cerebral palsy who have IQ's below 70 is APPROXIMATELY
    A. 30%
    B. 50%
    C. 70%
    D. 90%

21. Considerable progress has been made in the outpatient treatment of the   21.____
    emotionally disturbed individual through the use of
    A. prefrontal lobotomy   B. chemotherapy
    C. shock treatment   D. hydrotherapy

22. Personality studies of physically handicapped persons and persons not so   22.____
    handicapped show that
    A. there is no significant difference in frequency of personality problems
       between the two groups
    B. the most frequent personality deviation of the physically handicapped
       person is withdrawing behavior
    C. persons with closely similar disabilities tend to develop similar personality
       structures
    D. nearly all physically handicapped persons exhibit evidence of personality
       difficulties

23. The MOST common reaction of the physically handicapped child to separation   23.____
    from the family because of hospitalization is
    A. depression   B. projection   C. regression   D. sublimation

24. Psychologists generally agree that, when an emotional handicap exists in   24.____
    a person who has a physical disability, the emotional handicap
    A. usually stems directly from the physical handicap
    B. is usually much the same in all persons with that particular physical
       disability
    C. does not stem directly from the disability, but has been mediated by social
       variables
    D. is apt to be extremely severe

25. The ability of physically handicapped individuals to cope satisfactorily with   25.____
    ridicule and other difficult situations
    A. depends largely on the attitudes of society toward the handicapped
    B. may be strengthened by special training in social techniques
    C. decreases as the handicapped individual matures
    D. is a function of the sex of the individual

KEY (CORRECT ANSWERS)

1.	D		11.	D
2.	C		12.	B
3.	B		13.	B
4.	D		14.	C
5.	B		15.	B
6.	D		16.	D
7.	B		17.	B
8.	A		18.	C
9.	D		19.	D
10.	B		20.	B

21. B
22. B
23. C
24. C
25. B

EXAMINATION SECTION
TEST 1

DIRECTIONS: Each question or incomplete statement is followed by several suggested answers or completions. Select the one that BEST answers the question or completes the statement. *PRINT THE LETTER OF THE CORRECT ANSWER IN THE SPACE AT THE RIGHT.*

1. According to psychoanalytic theory, the part of the personality which is in closest contact with reality is the

    A. id
    B. superego
    C. libido
    D. ego

2. An individual who gives socially acceptable reasons for his behavior, either verbally, by thought, or conduct, is adjusting through the use of

    A. rationalization
    B. sublimation
    C. retrogression
    D. displacement

3. Of the following statements, the MOST nearly correct one regarding the rate of mental growth is that

    A. there is a deceleration of the rate of growth with age
    B. there is an increase in the rate of growth with age
    C. mental growth is constant throughout the period of childhood
    D. mental growth is constant during adulthood

4. In early childhood, the individual tends to pattern himself on or to identify himself MOST generally with

    A. glamorous or romantic figures
    B. age contemporaries
    C. characters in movies or on TV
    D. parents or parent substitutes

5. With respect to physical growth, superior children as compared with children of average intelligence are

    A. slightly inferior
    B. above average
    C. slightly superior
    D. markedly inferior

6. A candidate in an examination says, "I passed the written and the performance tests, but they failed me in the interview." The mechanism of personality defense which he is employing is

    A. compensation
    B. sublimation
    C. identification
    D. projection

7. The psychological forces or needs that influence human behavior are labeled

    A. extrasensory
    B. generalized
    C. intrinsic
    D. extrinsic

8. Reactions of nail biting, grimacing, clawing, spitting, etc. in a fourth-grade child are usually considered symptomatic evidence of

    A. low intelligence
    B. psychological conflict
    C. hypothyroidism
    D. nervousness

9. The greatest "social distance" in boy-girl relationships has been found to be during the ages

   A. 13 to 17 years
   B. 9 to 13 years
   C. 5 to 9 years
   D. 2 to 5 years

10. According to available findings, the effect of deprivation of affection on intellectual development is MOST likely to appear in a curtailment of the

    A. speed of learning even when the task is rather simple
    B. ability to memorize new material
    C. ability to retain material, once it has been learned
    D. ability to conceptualize

11. Of the following, the one which would MOST likely indicate faulty emotional development in a girl of six is

    A. striving for perfection in all her work
    B. stronger liking for music than other school work
    C. little interest in doll play
    D. reluctance to engage in competitive sports

12. When a six-year-old child violates the standards of conduct of the group, the teacher should

    A. criticize him in the presence of the group
    B. accept his behavior as the expression of a deep need
    C. support him in order to alleviate his guilt feelings
    D. discourage his behavior by showing why it is wrong

13. A shy child is MOST likely to be fairly well adjusted if he has

    A. clearly defined interests
    B. marked intellectual ability
    C. obvious physical handicaps
    D. outstanding artistic talent

14. A kindergarten child shows habitual reluctance to undertake a new activity. This is BEST interpreted as evidence of

    A. an inability to cope with adult authority
    B. a general attitude of insecurity
    C. a specific fear conditioned in infancy
    D. a persevering and independent attitude

15. For a four-year-old child, the events of the present are

    A. less vivid than those of the past
    B. less vivid than those of the future
    C. more vivid than those of the past or future
    D. as vivid as those of the past or future

16. The "ideal self" represents what an individual

    A. believes he ought to be
    B. believes others ought to be
    C. knows he can be
    D. knows he cannot be

17. Girls generally prefer groups of girls and boys prefer groups of boys during

    A. early childhood   B. latency
    C. pre-adolescence   D. adolescence

18. The rate and pattern of early motor development are largely determined by

    A. experience   B. learning
    C. maturation   D. training

19. Which of the following books describes how parents and other adults can help youngsters overcome problems of an urban environment?

    A. YOUR ADOLESCENT, L. K. and Mary Frank
    B. STUDIES IN ADOLESCENCE, Robert E. Grinder
    C. IN DEFENSE OF YOUTH, by Earl C. Kelley
    D. THE AMERICAN TEENAGER, by H.H. Remmers and D.H. Radler

20. When a person has gained some insight into his own emotional behavior, usually following resolution of an acute conflict, we often describe him as having increased his range of

    A. emotional repression   B. affective mobility
    C. understanding   D. clinical synapses

21. Sibling rivalry is the term used to describe the competitive feeling between two or more individuals who

    A. are in the same school grade
    B. are children of the same parents
    C. have similar goals of achievement
    D. are in the same chronological age group

22. The mental mechanism of minimizing one's own faults and deficiencies by criticizing and blaming others is known as

    A. compensation   B. rationalization
    C. transference   D. projection

23. Etiology is concerned primarily with

    A. symptomology   B. racial origin
    C. causation   D. language facility

24. Syndrome is BEST defined as a

    A. form of obsession in which the subject sees himself as someone else
    B. form of neurosis in which the subject constantly compares himself with others
    C. cardiac condition which has no apparent organic basis
    D. constellation of symptoms which characteristically occur together in a specific ailment

25. Girls tend to be superior to boys of the same age in
    A. linguistic fluency
    B. speed of reaction time
    C. arithmetical reasoning
    D. most forms of perception

26. Of the following, a major recreational activity common to both 10- and 15-year-old boys and girls is
    A. going to the movies
    B. riding a bicycle
    C. watching athletic sports
    D. social dancing

27. In general, juvenile fiction comprises the major part of the reading choices of
    A. girls between 9 and 13
    B. boys of all ages
    C. girls of all ages
    D. boys between 12 and 16

28. The behavior of the typical adolescent is BEST described as characteristically
    A. stubborn and willful, showing disregard for strictures of family and society
    B. inconsistent, alternating between childish and adult reactions
    C. irresponsible, exhibiting lack of judgment and poor taste
    D. individualistic, reflecting indifference to approval from parents and peers

29. Of the following observed behavior symptoms, the one which may BEST be described as "regression" is the pupil's
    A. use of infantile speech and verbal expressions
    B. thrusting aside of present desires in order to avoid conflict in a direct solution of a problem
    C. attempt to dominate every situation in which he finds himself
    D. evasion of possible failure by selecting an easier goal

30. UNDERSTANDING GROUP BEHAVIOR OF BOYS AND GIRLS was written by
    A. Helen H. Jennings
    B. Ruth Cunningham
    C. Jane Waters
    D. Alice V. Crow

31. When we compare young children and adolescents with respect to the relative effectiveness of distributed and concentrated practice as a learning technique, we find that
    A. young children learn better by distributed practice; adolescents by concentrated practice
    B. young children learn better by concentrated practice; adolescents by distributed practice
    C. both young children and adolescents learn better by concentrated practice
    D. both young children and adolescents learn better by distributed practice

32. Research has demonstrated that there is an increase in racial prejudice during adolescence. Of the following, the factor that contributes MOST significantly to this increase is

A. dislike for deviants from norms of social groups
B. influence of parental opinion
C. segregation of groups in school and community
D. fear of economic pressure from minority groups

33. Of the following teachers, the one MOST liked by the largest number of junior high school pupils is the one who

    A. sets easily attainable standards
    B. demonstrates a high level of intellectual competence
    C. maintains an impersonal, objective attitude
    D. is sympathetic

34. Of the following, the behavior which would be considered MOST indicative of potential or actual maladjustment in a junior high school boy is

    A. treating his classmates to sodas in an attempt to buy their votes in a school election
    B. spending his entire allowance each week on science fiction paperbacks
    C. finding fault with the work of his classmates
    D. failing to take care of school property

35. The proportion of TREATED juvenile delinquents who exhibit subsequent histories of failure to adjust to society is about

    A. 5%   B. 25%   C. 45%   D. 65%

36. Current evidence and thinking on the causative factors in juvenile delinquency support the view that

    A. social factors are more basic than psychological factor
    B. psychological factors are more basic than social factor
    C. psychological factors and social factors are of about equal importance
    D. physiological factors are more important than either social or psychological factors

37. Studies involving the relative mental abilities of delinquent and non-delinquent children have generally

    A. shown that there are no significant differences between them
    B. shown that delinquent children are slightly but significantly brighter than non-delinquents
    C. shown that non-delinquent children are somewhat brighter than delinquent children
    D. been about evenly divided some finding the delinquent children brighter, others finding mental superiority for non-delinquents

38. Separation of the infant from his mother can be a traumatic experience. The amount of emotional damage to the infant and the consequent effects on his personality depend MAINLY on the

    A. quality and consistency of the substitute mothering he receives
    B. reasons for and duration of the separation
    C. kind of preparation for separation the infant receives
    D. degree of the mother's acceptance of the placement

39. Research studies of language development in young children have shown that
    A. the multiple mothering of children in a large family delays language development
    B. language delay in otherwise normal children is usually related to inadequate language stimulation
    C. language delay is always associated with slow motor development
    D. children are usually slow in learning to talk when more than one language is spoken in the home

40. The two MOST important influences on the cultural development of a seven-year-old child are the
    A. home and peer group
    B. school and peer group
    C. home and school
    D. home and church

41. In our culture, a child gains his sense of identity MAINLY from
    A. knowledge about and experience with his parents and extended family
    B. association with members of his own ethnic group
    C. a study of the historical and ethnic factors in this culture
    D. association with his peers

42. Of the following, the MOST important influence on the personality development of a child during the first year is the
    A. family as a whole
    B. mother
    C. way his siblings react to him
    D. relationship between the parents

43. Of the following, the term which is generally applied to the situation in which an infant in foster care has insufficient interaction with a substitute mother is
    A. maternal rejection
    B. mothering complex
    C. maternal deprivation
    D. interaction deficiency

44. The normal four-year-old child should be expected to
    A. cut her meat with a knife
    B. bathe herself without help
    C. care for herself at the toilet
    D. tell time to the nearest quarter hour

45. It is usually not a good idea to take a child under the age of five to a movie that may frighten him MAINLY because young children cannot
    A. appreciate a cultural experience
    B. behave themselves in a movie theater
    C. distinguish clearly between real life and make believe
    D. see movies without acting out what they see

46. The average five-year-old child spends the MAJOR part of his play time

    A. playing by himself
    B. watching other children play
    C. playing cooperatively with other children
    D. playing competitive games involving teams

47. A children's counselor faced with a question about sex from a six-year-old child in her group should

    A. tell the child she is too young to understand such things
    B. give the child as honest and simple an answer as possible
    C. realize that an older child must have told the six-year-old to ask that question
    D. answer the question in such a way as to discourage the child from asking any more questions about sex

48. Most studies of children's fears indicate that fears of the supernatural are MOST common among the

    A. pre-schoolers   B. latency-age group
    C. pre-adolescents   D. adolescents

49. The boy who trips on the leg of a chair and then accuses the chair is using the mechanism of

    A. rationalization   B. regression
    C. daydreaming   D. projection

50. Mild amounts of emotion, such as anxiety, irritation, and apprehension, tend to have which of the following influences on learning and performance?

    A. Integrative   B. Mildly disintegrative
    C. Disruptive   D. Relatively little influence

KEY (CORRECT ANSWERS)

1. D	11. A	21. B	31. D	41. A
2. A	12. D	22. D	32. A	42. B
3. A	13. A	23. C	33. D	43. C
4. D	14. B	24. D	34. C	44. C
5. C	15. C	25. A	35. B	45. C
6. D	16. A	26. A	36. B	46. C
7. C	17. B	27. A	37. C	47. B
8. B	18. C	28. B	38. A	48. B
9. B	19. C	29. A	39. B	49. D
10. D	20. B	30. B	40. C	50. A

TEST 2

DIRECTIONS: Each question or incomplete statement is followed by several suggested answers or completions. Select the one that BEST answers the question or completes the statement. *PRINT THE LETTER OF THE CORRECT ANSWER IN THE SPACE AT THE RIGHT.*

1. The process by which children take to themselves the values, the thinking, and the social behavior of their parents is known as

    A. projection
    B. identification
    C. denigration
    D. sublimation
    E. imitation

2. An understanding of the family relationships of a youngster who presents a problem of under-achievement

    A. is worthwhile but not essential
    B. is important but not within the province of the teacher
    C. may reveal factors that have an important bearing on his problem
    D. is unlikely to be related to the difficulties the young person has with his school work
    E. is important but not within the province of the guidance counselor

3. Which of the following is the MOST correct statement concerning puberty and physical maturity?

    A. Boys and girls who experience early puberty will achieve physical maturity and cease growing later than will the late maturers.
    B. Boys and girls who experience early puberty will achieve physical maturity and cease growing sooner than will the late maturers.
    C. Boys and girls who experience early puberty will achieve physical maturity and cease growing at approximately the same time as the late maturers.
    D. Boys and girls who experience early puberty will achieve physical maturity and cease growing in any standard pattern, together with the late maturers.
    E. None of the above.

4. The MOST prominent difficulties of the middle years of childhood revolve around

    A. relations with peer groups
    B. parent-child relationships
    C. schooling and the ability to learn
    D. physical development
    E. emotional and spiritual development

5. The MOST accurate statement concerning anxiety, of the following, is that anxiety is

    A. needed for the socialization process
    B. not needed for the socialization process
    C. less produced by "mental" punishment than by physical punishment
    D. of negligible effect in producing neurosis
    E. neutralized by feelings of guilt and inadequacy

6. Most studies of children's fears indicate that fears of the supernatural are MOST common among the

   A. early childhood group
   B. latency-age group
   C. pre-teen group
   D. adolescents
   E. early childhood group and adolescents as contrasted with the pre-teen and latency-age groups

7. The boy who trips on the leg of a chair and then accuses the chair is using the mechanism of

   A. rationalization   B. regression
   C. sublimation   D. projection
   E. delusion

8. Mild amounts of emotion, such as anxiety, irritation, and apprehension, tend to have which of the following influences on learning and performance?

   A. Integrative   B. Mildly disintegrative
   C. Disruptive   D. Integrative and segregative
   E. Disruptive and disintegrative

9. The "ideal self" represents what an individual

   A. believes he ought to be
   B. believes others ought to be
   C. knows he can be
   D. knows others can be
   E. believes he ought to be and can be

10. Girls generally prefer groups of girls AND boys prefer groups of boys during

    A. early childhood
    B. latency
    C. pre-adolescence
    D. adolescence
    E. early childhood and pre-adolescence

11. The rate and pattern of early motor development are largely determined by

    A. experience   B. learning
    C. maturation   D. training
    E. practice

12. Changes in cognitive behavior between childhood and adolescence are in the direction of greater

    A. understanding of abstractions
    B. reliance on concrete realities
    C. dependence on vicarious experiences
    D. emphasis on intuition
    E. collection of scattered peripheral details

13. Gesell refers to the child's development between the ages of six and ten as   13.____

    A. an ever-widening spiral   B. a task phase
    C. a latency period   D. a transitional interval
    E. an imitative stage

14. A defense mechanism defined as the adoption of an attitude opposite to one that pre-   14.____
    cedes anxiety is

    A. sophistry   B. reaction formation
    C. fantasy   D. verification
    E. rationalization

15. Experiments with the reactions of varying age groups to snakes indicated that, in gen-   15.____
    eral, the greatest fear was exhibited by

    A. infants   B. primary pupils
    C. latency-age children   D. adolescents
    E. E. adults

16. As children get older, the differences in ability between the bright and the dull tend to   16.____

    A. become smaller
    B. become larger
    C. remain about the same
    D. vary in no set pattern
    E. become larger, level off, and then become smaller

17. Which one of the following descriptions is characteristic of the actively-rejected home?   17.____

    A. Parents show highly emotional attitude, warmth without understanding.
    B. Parents tend to use severe punishment only if irritated.
    C. Parents restrict child's independence with many rules and requirements.
    D. Child is expected to make his own decisions, although advice is unavailable.
    E. Parents are jealous of, and in active competition with, their children.

18. Homesickness is an example of which type of adjustment mechanism?   18.____

    A. Guilt   B. Identification
    C. Reaction   D. Sublimation
    E. Regression

19. Children below the age of 10 when asked to write on "The person I would like to be" most   19.____
    frequently want to vie with

    A. peers   B. older siblings
    C. parents   D. real or imaginary heroes
    E. teachers

20. When a child strikes out at a person who did not provoke the anger, the child is exhibiting   20.____

    A. depression   B. retrogression
    C. compensation   D. displaced aggression
    E. projection

21. Which of the following statements describes the effect upon intellectually gifted children of early school entrance and acceleration?   21._____

    A. It serves to delay their social development.
    B. It produces underachievers.
    C. It creates emotional problems.
    D. It leads to favorable and valuable results.
    E. It substantially affects the development of motor skills.

22. The psychological forces or needs that influence human behavior are labeled   22._____

    A. extrasensory
    B. extrinsic
    C. intrinsic
    D. generalized
    E. contingent

23. Reactions of nail biting, grimacing, clawing, spitting, etc. in a fourth-grade child are usually considered symptomatic evidence of   23._____

    A. anxiety
    B. dementia
    C. low intelligence
    D. hypothyroidism
    E. psychological conflict

24. An individual who gives socially acceptable reasons for his behavior, either verbally, by thought, or conduct, is adjusting through the use of   24._____

    A. rationalization
    B. displacement
    C. sublimation
    D. retrogression
    E. projection

25. Of the following statements, the MOST NEARLY correct one regarding the rate of mental growth is that   25._____

    A. there is a deceleration of the rate of growth with age
    B. mental growth is constant during adulthood
    C. mental growth is constant throughout the period of childhood
    D. there is an increase in the rate of growth with age
    E. the rate of mental growth increases and decreases in a standard pattern

26. In early childhood, the individual tends to pattern himself on or to identify himself MOST generally with   26._____

    A. glamorous or romantic figures
    B. age contemporaries
    C. characters in movies or on TV
    D. parents or parent substitutes
    E. older siblings

27. With respect to physical growth, mentally superior children as compared with children of average intelligence are   27._____

    A. markedly inferior
    B. slightly inferior
    C. slightly superior
    D. markedly superior
    E. about average

28. A candidate in an examination says, "I passed the written and the performance tests, but they failed me in the interview." The mechanism of personality defense which he is employing is

   A. compensation
   B. sublimation
   C. identification
   D. projection
   E. rationalization

29. The psychologist whose name is MOST often associated with the theory that the experience of birth has a profound influence on personality development and that an individual who has a slow, prolonged birth is likely to have a personality which fights, struggles and plunges is

   A. Horney
   B. Freud
   C. Sullivan
   D. Rank
   E. McDougall

30. Two different studies have suggested that children who will probably have lower I.Q.'s are those who have been reared in

   A. institutions
   B. broken homes
   C. foster homes
   D. upper class homes
   E. lower class homes

31. Studies of twins reared together indicate that the correlation coefficients of intelligence tests scores for identical twins lie in the range of

   A. .40-.55
   B. .65-.74
   C. .75-.79
   D. .80-.90
   E. .90-1.00

32. As a means of changing the current behavior pattern of an adolescent, which of the following forces will generally prove to be MOST potent? Disapproval of the behavior pattern by

   A. the adolescent's parents
   B. an adult he admires
   C. a group of his peers
   D. his classroom teacher
   E. older siblings

33. If the results of studies of boys' clubs are applicable to the school situation, one may expect the greatest amount of aggressive behavior to be noted in classes where the classroom climate may be described as

   A. permissive
   B. laissez-faire
   C. democratic
   D. autocratic
   E. unstructured

34. Of the following, the LEAST effective way of dealing with children's fears is

   A. explaining and reassuring
   B. helping the child to face the feared situation
   C. simply ignoring the child's fears
   D. setting examples of fearlessness
   E. removing the cause of fear from the child's environment

35. The age at which individuals cease to grow in intellectual ability is   35.____

    A. 13 years   B. 16 years
    C. 21 years   D. 35 years
    E. probably none of these

36. The theory that physical compensation for a feeling of physical or social inferiority is   36.____
    responsible for the development of a psychoneurosis is attributed to

    A. Adler   B. Horney
    C. Freud   D. Sullivan
    E. Jung

37. Which of the following terms refers to the maintenance of stability in the physiological   37.____
    functioning of the organism?

    A. functional autonomy   B. canalization
    C. homeostasis   D. maturation
    E. physiological integration

38. Which of the following authors would you be LEAST likely to recommend for information   38.____
    about child care?

    A. Sidonie Gruenberg   B. Jean Piaget
    C. Ernest Harms   D. Benjamin Spock
    E. Arnold Gesell

39. All of the following statements are generally TRUE of children of elementary school age   39.____
    EXCEPT

    A. girls mature approximately one year earlier than do boys
    B. girls have poorer health than boys
    C. girls excel in body balance and fine hand coordination
    D. girls excel in school achievement
    E. girls tend to get their second set of teeth earlier than boys

40. The teacher of a sixth-grade class is likely to find all of the following characteristics   40.____
    among children of this growth level EXCEPT that they

    A. are influenced very little by what their peers do
    B. are beginning to rebel against adult domination
    C. are at a receptive stage for indoctrination of all sorts
    D. enjoy giving assistance to younger children in the lower grades
    E. are beginning to show more discrimination in the selection of possessions and in
       the care of them

KEY (CORRECT ANSWERS)

1.	B	11.	C	21.	D	31.	D
2.	C	12.	A	22.	C	32.	C
3.	B	13.	A	23.	E	33.	D
4.	C	14.	B	24.	A	34.	C
5.	A	15.	E	25.	A	35.	E
6.	B	16.	B	26.	D	36.	A
7.	D	17.	C	27.	C	37.	C
8.	A	18.	E	28.	D	38.	B
9.	A	19.	C	29.	D	39.	B
10.	B	20.	D	30.	A	40.	A

REPORT WRITING
EXAMINATION SECTION
TEST 1

DIRECTIONS: Each question or incomplete statement is followed by several suggested answers or completions. Select the one that BEST answers the question or completes the statement. *PRINT THE LETTER OF THE CORRECT ANSWER IN THE SPACE AT THE RIGHT.*

Questions 1-4.

DIRECTIONS: Answer Questions 1 through 4 on the basis of the following report which was prepared by a supervisor for inclusion in his agency's annual report.

Line #
1 On Oct. 13, I was assigned to study the salaries paid.
2 to clerical employees in various titles by the city and by
3 private industry in the area.
4 In order to get the data I needed, I called Mr. Johnson at
5 the Bureau of the Budget and the payroll officers at X Corp.—
6 a brokerage house, Y Co. —an insurance company, and Z Inc. —
7 a publishing firm. None of them was available and I had to call
8 all of them again the next day.
9 When I finally got the information I needed, I drew up a
10 chart, which is attached. Note that not all of the companies I
11 contacted employed people at all the different levels used in the
12 city service.
13 The conclusions I draw from analyzing this information is
14 as follows: The city's entry-level salary is about average for
15 the region; middle-level salaries are generally higher in the
16 city government plan than in private industry; but salaries at the
17 highest levels in private industry are better than city em-
18 ployees' pay.

1. Which of the following criticisms about the style in which this report is written is MOST valid?   1.____
   A. It is too informal.
   B. It is too concise.
   C. It is too choppy.
   D. The syntax is too complex.

2. Judging from the statements made in the report, the method followed by this employee in performing his research was   2.____
   A. *good*; he contacted a representative sample of businesses in the area
   B. *poor*; he should have drawn more definite conclusions
   C. *good*; he was persistent in collecting information
   D. *poor*; he did not make a thorough study

3. One sentence in this report contains a grammatical error. This sentence begins on line number
   A. 4   B. 7   C. 10   D. 14

4. The type of information given in this report which should be presented in footnotes or in an appendix is the
   A. purpose of the study
   B. specifics about the businesses contacted
   C. reference to the chart
   D. conclusions drawn by the author

5. The use of a graph to show statistical data in a report is SUPERIOR to a table because it
   A. features approximations
   B. emphasizes facts and relationships more dramatically
   C. presents data more accurately
   D. is easily understood by the average reader

6. Of the following, the degree of formality required of a written report in tone is MOST likely to depend on the
   A. subject matter of the report
   B. frequency of its occurrence
   C. amount of time available for its preparation
   D. audience for whom the report is intended

7. Of the following, a distinguishing characteristic of a written report intended for the head of your agency as compared to a report prepared for a lower-echelon staff member is that the report for the agency head should USUALLY include
   A. considerably more detail, especially statistical data
   B. the essential details in an abbreviated form
   C. all available source material
   D. an annotated bibliography

8. Assume that you are asked to write a lengthy report for use by the administrator of your agency, the subject of which is "The Impact of Proposed New Data Processing Operation on Line Personnel" in your agency. You decide that the *most* appropriate type of report for you to prepare is an analytical report, including recommendations.
   The MAIN reason for your decision is that
   A. the subject of the report is extremely complex
   B. large sums of money are involved
   C. the report is being prepared for the administrator
   D. you intend to include charts and graphs

9. Assume that you are preparing a report based on a survey dealing with the attitudes of employees in Division X regarding proposed new changes in compensating employees for working overtime. Three percent of the respondents to the survey voluntarily offer an unfavorable opinion on the method of assigning overtime work, a question not specifically asked of the employees.
On the basis of this information, the MOST appropriate and significant of the following comments for you to make in the report with regard to employees' attitudes on assigning overtime work is that
   A. an insignificant percentage of employees dislike the method of assigning overtime work
   B. three percent of the employees in Division X dislike the method of assigning overtime work
   C. three percent of the sample selected for the survey voiced an unfavorable opinion on the method of assigning overtime work
   D. some employees voluntarily voiced negative feelings about the method of assigning overtime work, making it impossible to determine the extent of this attitude

10. A supervisor should be able to prepare a report that is well-written and unambiguous.
Of the following sentences that might appear in a report, select the one which communicates MOST clearly the intent of its author.
   A. When your subordinates speak to a group of people, they should be well-informed.
   B. When he asked him to leave, SanMan King told him that he would refuse the request.
   C. Because he is a good worker, Foreman Jefferson assigned Assistant Foreman D'Agostino to replace him.
   D. Each of us is responsible for the actions of our subordinates.

11. In some reports, especially longer ones, a list of the resources (books, papers, magazines, etc.) used to prepare it is included. This list is called the
   A. accreditation   B. bibliography
   C. summary   D. glossary

12. Reports are usually divided into several sections, some of which are more necessary than others.
Of the following, the section which is ABSOLUTELY necessary to include in a report is
   A. a table of contents   B. the body
   C. an index   D. a bibliography

13. Suppose you are writing a report on an interview you have just completed with a particularly hostile applicant.
Which of the following BEST describes what you should include in this report?
    A. What you think caused the applicant's hostile attitude during the interview
    B. Specific examples of the applicant's hostile remarks and behavior
    C. The relevant information uncovered during the interview
    D. A recommendation that the applicant's request be denied because of his hostility

14. When including recommendations in a report to your supervisor, which of the following is MOST important for you to do?
    A. Provide several alternative courses of action for each recommendation
    B. First present the supporting evidence, then the recommendations
    C. First present the recommendations, then the supporting evidence
    D. Make sure the recommendations arise logically out of the information in the report

15. It is often necessary that the writer of a report present facts and sufficient arguments to gain acceptance of the points, conclusions, or recommendations set forth in the report.
Of the following, the LEAST advisable step to take in organizing a report, when such argumentation is the important factor, is a(n)
    A. elaborate expression of personal belief
    B. businesslike discussion of the problem as a whole
    C. orderly arrangement of convincing data
    D. reasonable explanation of the primary issues

16. In some types of reports, visual aids add interest, meaning, and support. They also provide an essential means of effectively communicating the message of the report.
Of the following, the selection of the suitable visual aids to use with a report is LEAST dependent on the
    A. nature and scope of the report
    B. way in which the aid is to be used
    C. aid used in other reports
    D. prospective readers of the report

17. Visual aids used in a report may be placed either in the text material or in the appendix.
Deciding where to put a chart, table, or any such aid should depend on the
    A. title of the report   B. purpose of the visual aid
    C. title of the visual aid   D. length of the report

18. A report is often revised several times before final preparation and distribution in an effort to make certain the report meets the needs of the situation for which it is designed.
Which of the following is the BEST way for the author to be sure that a report covers the areas he intended?

A. Obtain a coworker's opinion
B. Compare it with a content checklist
C. Test it on a subordinate
D. Check his bibliography

19. In which of the following situations is an oral report preferable to a written report? When a(n)
    A. recommendation is being made for a future plan of action
    B. department head requests immediate information
    C. long-standing policy change is made
    D. analysis of complicated statistical data is involved

    19._____

20. When an applicant is approved, the supervisor must fill in standard forms with certain information.
    The GREATEST advantage of using standard forms in this situation rather than having the supervisor write the report as he sees fit is that
    A. the report can be acted on quickly
    B. the report can be written without directions from a supervisor
    C. needed information is less likely to be left out of the report
    D. information that is written up this way is more likely to be verified

    20._____

21. Assume that it is part of your job to prepare a monthly report for your unit head that eventually goes to the director. The report contains information on the number of applicants you have interviewed that have been approved and the number of applicants you have interviewed that have been turned down.
    Errors on such reports are serious because
    A. you are expected to be able to prove how many applicants you have interviewed each month
    B. accurate statistics are needed for effective management of the department
    C. they may not be discovered before the report is transmitted to the director
    D. they may result in loss to the applicants left out of the report

    21._____

22. The frequency with which job reports are submitted should depend MAINLY on
    A. how comprehensive the report has to be
    B. the amount of information in the report
    C. the availability of an experienced man to write the report
    D. the importance of changes in the information included in the report

    22._____

23. The CHIEF purpose in preparing an outline for a report is usually to insure that
    A. the report will be grammatically correct
    B. every point will be given equal emphasis
    C. principal and secondary points will be properly integrated
    D. the language of the report will be of the same level and include the same technical terms

    23._____

24. The MAIN reason for requiring written job reports is to 24.____
    A. avoid the necessity of oral orders
    B. develop better methods of doing the work
    C. provide a permanent record of what was done
    D. increase the amount of work that can be done

25. Assume you are recommending in a report to your supervisor that a radical 25.____
    change in a standard maintenance procedure should be adopted.
    Of the following, the MOST important information to be included in this report is
    A. a list of the reasons for making this change
    B. the names of others who favor the change
    C. a complete description of the present procedure
    D. amount of training time needed for the new procedure

KEY (CORRECT ANSWERS)

1.	A		11.	B
2.	D		12.	B
3.	D		13.	C
4.	B		14.	D
5.	B		15.	A
6.	D		16.	C
7.	B		17.	B
8.	A		18.	B
9.	D		19.	B
10.	D		20.	C

21. B
22. D
23. C
24. C
25. A

TEST 2

DIRECTIONS: Each question or incomplete statement is followed by several suggested answers or completions. Select the one that BEST answers the question or completes the statement. *PRINT THE LETTER OF THE CORRECT ANSWER IN THE SPACE AT THE RIGHT.*

1. It is often necessary that the writer of a report present facts and sufficient arguments to gain acceptance of the points, conclusions, or recommendations set forth in the report.
   Of the following, the LEAST advisable step to take in organizing a report, when such argumentation is the important factor, is a(n)
   A. elaborate expression of personal belief
   B. businesslike discussion of the problem as a whole
   C. orderly arrangement of convincing data
   D. reasonable explanation of the primary issues

   1.____

2. Of the following, the factor which is generally considered to be LEAST characteristic of a good control report is that it
   A. stresses performance that adheres to standard rather than emphasizing the exception
   B. supplies information intended to serve as the basis for corrective action
   C. provides feedback for the planning process
   D. includes data that reflect trends as well as current status

   2.____

3. An administrative assistant has been asked by his superior to write a concise, factual report with objective conclusions and recommendations based on facts assembled by other researchers.
   Of the following factors, the administrative assistant should give LEAST consideration to
   A. the educational level of the person or persons for whom the report is being prepared
   B. the use to be made of the report
   C. the complexity of the problem
   D. his own feelings about the importance of the problem

   3.____

4. When making a written report, it is often recommended that the findings or conclusions be presented near the beginning of the report.
   Of the following, the MOST important reason for doing this is that it
   A. facilitates organizing the material clearly
   B. assures that all the topics will be covered
   C. avoids unnecessary repetition of ideas
   D. prepares the reader for the facts that will follow

   4.____

5. You have been asked to write a report on methods of hiring and training new employees. Your report is going to be about ten pages long.
   For the convenience of your readers, a brief summary of your findings should
   A. appear at the beginning of your report
   B. be appended to the report as a postscript
   C. be circulated in a separate memo
   D. be inserted in tabular form in the middle of your report

6. In preparing a report, the MAIN reason for writing an outline is usually to
   A. help organize thoughts in a logical sequence
   B. provide a guide for the typing of the report
   C. allow the ultimate user to review the report in advance
   D. ensure that the report is being prepared on schedule

7. The one of the following which is MOST appropriate as a reason for including footnotes in a report is to
   A. correct capitalization
   B. delete passages
   C. improve punctuation
   D. cite references

8. A completed formal report may contain all of the following EXCEPT
   A. a synopsis
   B. a preface
   C. marginal notes
   D. bibliographical references

9. Of the following, the MAIN use of proofreaders' marks is to
   A. explain corrections to be made
   B. indicate that a manuscript has been read and approved
   C. let the reader know who proofread the report
   D. indicate the format of the report

10. Informative, readable, and concise reports have been found to observe the following rules:
    Rule I.   Keep the report short and easy to understand
    Rule II. Vary the length of sentences.
    Rule III. Vary the style of sentences so that, for example, they are not all just subject-verb, subject-verb.
    Consider this hospital laboratory report: The experiment was started in January. The apparatus was put together in six weeks. At that time, the synthesizing process was begun. The synthetic chemicals were separated. Then they were used in tests on patients.
    Which one of the following choices MOST accurately classifies the above rules into those which are violated by this report ad those which are not?
    A. II is violated, but I and III are not.
    B. III is violated, but I and II are not.
    C. II and III are violated, but I is not.
    D. I, II, and III are violated,

Questions 11-13.

DIRECTIONS: Questions 11 through 13 are based on the following example of a report. The report consists of eight numbered sentences, some of which are not consistent with the principles of good report writing.

(1) I interviewed Mrs. Loretta Crawford in Room 424 of County Hospital. (2) She had collapsed on the street and been brought into emergency. (3) She is an attractive woman with many friends judging by the cards she had received. (4) She did not know what her husband's last job had been, or what their present income was. (5) The first thing that Mrs. Crawford said was that she had never worked and that her husband was presently unemployed. (6) She did not know if they had any medical coverage or if they could pay the bill. (7) She said that her husband could not be reached by telephone but that he would be in to see her that afternoon. (8) I left word at the nursing station to be called when he arrived.

11. A good report should be arranged in logical order.
 Which of the following sentences from the report does NOT appear in its proper sequence in the report?
 A. 1 B. 4 C. 7 D. 8

12. Only material that is relevant to the main thought of a report should be included.
 Which of the following sentences from the report contains material which is LEAST relevant to this report? Sentence
 A. 3 B. 4 C. 6 D. 8

13. Reports should include all essential information.
 Of the following, the MOST important fact that is missing from this report is:
 A. Who was involved in the interview
 B. What was discovered at the interview
 C. When the interview took place
 D. Where the interview took place

Questions 14-15.

DIRECTIONS: Each of Questions 14 and 15 consists of four numbered sentences which constitute a paragraph in a report. They are not in the right order. Choose the numbered arrangement appearing after letter A, B, C, or D which is MOST logical and which BEST expresses the thought of the paragraph.

14. I. Congress made the commitment explicit in the Housing Act of 1949, establishing as a national goal the realization of a decent home and suitable environment for every American family.
 II. The result has been that the goal of decent home and suitable environment is still as far distant as ever for the disadvantaged urban family
 III. In spite of this action by Congress, federal housing programs have continued to be fragmented and grossly under-funded.
 IV. The passage of the National Housing Act signaled a new federal commitment to provide housing for the nation's citizens.

The CORRECT answer is:
A. I, IV, III, II B. IV, I, III, II C. IV, I, III, II D. II, IV, I, III

15. I. The greater expense does not necessarily involve "exploitation," but it is often perceived as exploitative and unfair by those who are aware of the price differences involved, but unaware of operating costs.
    II. Ghetto residents believe they are "exploited" by local merchants, and evidence substantiates some of these beliefs.
    III. However, stores in low-income areas were more likely to be small independents, which could not achieve the economies available to supermarket chains and were, therefore, more likely to charge higher prices, and the customers were more likely to buy smaller-sized packages which are more expensive per unit of measure.
    IV. A study conducted in one city showed that distinctly higher prices were charged for goods sold in ghetto stores than in other areas.

    The CORRECT answer is:
    A. IV, II, I, III B. IV, I, III, II C. II, IV, III, I D. II, III, IV, I

16. In organizing data to be presented in a formal report, the FIRST of the following steps should be
    A. determining the conclusions to be drawn
    B. establishing the time sequence of the data
    C. sorting and arranging like data into groups
    D. evaluating how consistently the data support the recommendations

17. All reports should be prepared with at least one copy so that
    A. there is one copy for your file
    B. there is a copy for your supervisor
    C. the report can be sent to more than one person
    D. the person getting the report can forward a copy to someone else

18. Before turning in a report of an investigation he has made, a supervisor discovers some additional information he did not include in this report. Whether he rewrites this report to include this additional information should PRIMARILY depend on the
    A. importance of the report itself
    B. number of people who will eventually review this report
    C. established policy covering the subject matter of the report
    D. bearing this new information has on the conclusions of the report

KEY (CORRECT ANSWERS)

1.	A	11.	B
2.	A	12.	A
3.	D	13.	C
4.	D	14.	B
5.	A	15.	C
6.	A	16.	C
7.	D	17.	A
8.	C	18.	D
9.	A		
10.	C		

DOCUMENTS AND FORMS
PREPARING WRITTEN MATERIALS
EXAMINATION SECTION
TEST 1

DIRECTIONS: Each question or incomplete statement is followed by several suggested answers or completions. Select the one that BEST answers the question or completes the statement. *PRINT THE LETTER OF THE CORRECT ANSWER IN THE SPACE AT THE RIGHT.*

1. Of the following forms, the one in which horizontal lines may BEST be omitted is one 1.____

    A. that is to be filled in by hand
    B. that is to be filled in by typewriter
    C. which requires many fill-ins
    D. with little room for fill-ins

2. A certain form letter starts with the words *Dear Mr.* followed by a blank space. 2.____
    The MAJOR shortcoming in this is that

    A. salutations should not be placed on form letters
    B. *Gentlemen:* is preferable in a formal business letter
    C. the name will have to be typed in
    D. this salutation may be inappropriate

3. *Form paragraphs* may BEST be defined as 3.____

    A. block-style paragraphs
    B. paragraphs on a form
    C. paragraphs within a form letter
    D. standardized paragraphs used in correspondence

4. In general, the CHIEF economy of using multicopy forms is in 4.____

    A. the paper on which the form is printed
    B. printing the form
    C. employee time
    D. carbon paper

5. Suppose your supervisor has asked you to develop a form to record certain information needed. 5.____
    The FIRST thing you should do is to

    A. determine the type of data that will be recorded repeatedly so that it can be preprinted
    B. study the relationship of the form to the job to be accomplished so that the form can be planned
    C. determine the information that will be recorded in the same place on each copy of the form so that it can be used as a check
    D. find out who will be responsible for supplying the information so that space can be provided for their signatures

6. Which of the following is MOST likely to reduce the volume of paperwork in a unit responsible for preparing a large number of reports?

   A. Changing the office layout so that there will be a minimum of backtracking and delay
   B. Acquiring additional adding and calculating machines
   C. Consolidating some of the reports
   D. Inaugurating a *records retention* policy to reduce the length of time office papers are retained

7. Of the following basic guides to effective letter writing, which one would NOT be recommended as a way of improving the quality of business letters?

   A. Use emphatic phrases like *close proximity* and *first and foremost* to round out sentences.
   B. Break up complicated sentences by making short sentences out of dependent clauses.
   C. Replace old-fashioned phrases like *enclosed please find* and *recent date* with a more direct approach.
   D. Personalize letters by using your reader's name at least once in the body of the message.

8. Suppose that you must write a reply letter to a citizen's request for a certain pamphlet printed by your agency. The pamphlet is temporarily unavailable but a new supply will be arriving by December 8 or 9.
   Of the following four sentences, which one expresses the MOST positive business letter writing approach?

   A. We cannot send the materials you requested until after December 8.
   B. May we assure you that the materials you requested will be sent as quickly as possible.
   C. We will be sending the materials you requested as soon as our supply is replenished.
   D. We will mail the materials you requested on or shortly after December 8.

9. Using form letters in business correspondence is LEAST effective when

   A. answering letters on a frequently recurring subject
   B. giving the same information to many addresses
   C. the recipient is only interested in the routine information contained in the form letter
   D. a reply must be keyed to the individual requirements of the intended reader

10. The ability to write memos and letters is very important in clerical and administrative work. Methodical planning of a reply letter usually involves the following basic steps which are arranged in random order:
    I. Determine the purpose of the letter you are about to write.
    II. Make an outline of what information your reply letter should contain.
    III. Read carefully the letter to be answered to find out its main points.
    IV. Assemble the facts to be included in your reply letter.
    V. Visualize your intended reader and adapt your letter writing style to him.
    If the above numbered steps were arranged in their proper logical order, the one which would be THIRD in the sequence is

    A. II   B. III   C. IV   D. V

11. Generally, the frequency with which reports are to be submitted or the length of the interval which they cover should depend MAINLY on the

    A. amount of time needed to prepare the reports
    B. degree of comprehensiveness required in the reports
    C. availability of the data to be included in the reports
    D. extent of the variations in the data with the passage of time

12. The objectiveness of a report is its unbiased presentation of the facts.
    If this is so, which of the following reports listed below is likely to be the MOST objective?

    A. The Best Use of an Electronic Computer in Department Z
    B. The Case for Raising the Salaries of Employees in Department A
    C. Quarterly Summary of Production in the Duplicating Unit of Department Y
    D. Recommendation to Terminate Employee X's Services Because of Misconduct

13. Of the following, the MOST effective report writing style is usually characterized by

    A. covering all the main ideas in the same paragraph
    B. presenting each significant point in a new paragraph
    C. placing the least important points before the most important points
    D. giving all points equal emphasis throughout the report

14. Of the following, which factor is COMMON to all types of reports?

    A. Presentation of information
    B. Interpretation of findings
    C. Chronological ordering of the information
    D. Presentation of conclusions and recommendations

15. When writing a report, the one of the following which you should do FIRST is

    A. set up a logical work schedule
    B. determine your objectives in writing the report
    C. select your statistical material
    D. obtain the necessary data from the files

16. Good report writing utilizes, where possible, the use of table of contents, clear titles and sub-titles, well-labeled tables and figures, and good summaries in prominent places.
    These features in a report are MOST helpful in

    A. saving the reader's time
    B. emphasizing objectivity
    C. providing a basic reference tool
    D. forming a basis for future action

17. The one of the following which BEST describes a periodic report is that it

    A. provides a record of accomplishments for a given time span and a comparison with similar time spans in the past
    B. covers the progress made in a project that has been postponed
    C. integrates, summarizes, and perhaps interprets published data on technical or scientific material
    D. describes a decision, advocates a policy or action, and presents facts in support of the writer's position

18. The PRIMARY purpose of including pictorial illustrations in a formal report is usually to

   A. amplify information which has been adequately treated verbally
   B. present details that are difficult to describe verbally
   C. provide the reader with a pleasant, momentary distraction
   D. present supplementary information incidental to the main ideas developed in the report

19. Of the following, which is usually the MOST important guideline in writing business letters?
   A letter should be

   A. Neat
   B. Written in a formalized style
   C. Written in clear language intelligible to the reader
   D. Written in the past tense

20. Suppose you are asked to edit a policy statement. You note that personal pronouns like *you, we,* and *I* are used freely.
   Which of the following statements BEST applies to this use of personal pronouns?

   A. It is proper usage because written business language should not be different from carefully spoken business language.
   B. It requires correction because it is ungrammatical.
   C. It is proper because it is clearer and has a warmer tone.
   D. It requires correction because policies should be expressed in an impersonal manner.

21. Good business letters are coherent.
   To be coherent means to

   A. keep only one unifying idea in the message
   B. present the total message
   C. use simple, direct words for the message
   D. tie together the various ideas in the message

22. A functional forms file is a collection of forms which are grouped by

   A. purpose   B. department   C. title   D. subject

23. All of the following are reasons to consult a records retention schedule except one.
   Which one is that?
   To determine

   A. Whether something should be filed
   B. How long something should stay in file
   C. Who should be assigned to filing
   D. When something on file should be destroyed

24. A secretary is MOST likely to employ a form letter when 24.____
    A. an answer is not required
    B. the same information must be repeated from letter to letter
    C. there is not enough information to write a detailed reply
    D. varied correspondence must be sent out quickly

25. Of the following, the BASIC intent of naming a form is to provide the means to 25.____
    A. code those factors recorded on each form
    B. describe the use of the form
    C. index each form
    D. call attention to specific sections within each form

KEY (CORRECT ANSWERS)

1. B	11. D
2. D	12. C
3. D	13. B
4. C	14. A
5. B	15. B
6. C	16. A,C
7. A	17. A
8. D	18. B
9. D	19. C
10. A	20. D

21. D
22. A
23. C
24. B
25. B

TEST 2

DIRECTIONS: Each question or incomplete statement is followed by several suggested answers or completions. Select the one that BEST answers the question or completes the statement. *PRINT THE LETTER OF THE CORRECT ANSWER IN THE SPACE AT THE RIGHT.*

1. Assume that you are assigned the task of reducing the time and costs involved in completing a form that is frequently used in your agency. After analyzing the matter, you decide to reduce the writing requirements of the form through the use of ballot boxes and preprinted data.
   If exact copy-to-copy registration of this form is necessary, it is MOST advisable to

   A. vary the sizes of the ballot boxes
   B. stagger the ballot boxes
   C. place the ballot boxes as close together as possible
   D. have the ballot boxes follow the captions

2. To overcome problems that are involved in the use of cut-sheet and padded forms, specialty forms have been developed. Normally, these forms are commercially manufactured rather than produced in-plant. Before designing a form as a specialty form, however, you should be assured that certain factors are present.
   Which one of the following factors deserve LEAST consideration?

   A. The form is to be used in quantities of 5,000 or more annually.
   B. The forms will be prepared on equipment using either a pinfeed device or pressure rollers for continuous feed-through.
   C. Two or more copies of the form set must be held together for further processing subsequent to the initial distribution of the form set.
   D. Copies of the form will be identical, and no items of data will be selectively eliminated from one or more copies of the form.

3. Although a well-planned form should require little explanation as to its completion, there are many occasions when the analyst will find it necessary to include instructions on the form to assure that the person completing it does so correctly.
   With respect to such instructions, it is usually considered to be LEAST appropriate to place them

   A. in footnotes at the bottom of the form
   B. following the spaces to be completed
   C. directly under the form's title
   D. on the front of the form

4. One of the basic data-arrangement methods used in forms design is the *on-line* method. When this method is used, captions appear on the same line as the space provided for entry of the variable data.
   This arrangement is NOT recommended because it

   A. forces the typist to make use of the typewriter's tab stops, thus increasing processing time
   B. wastes horizontal space since the caption appears on the writing line
   C. tends to make the variable data become more dominant than the captions
   D. increases the form's processing time by requiring the typist to continually roll the platen back and forth to expose the caption

5. Of the following, the BEST reason for using form letters in correspondence is that they are

   A. concise and businesslike
   B. impersonal in tone
   C. uniform in appearance
   D. economical for large mailings

6. Of the following, the MOST important reason to sort large volumes of documents before filing is that sorting

   A. decreases the need for cross-referencing
   B. eliminates the need to keep the files up to date
   C. prevents overcrowding of the file drawers
   D. saves time and energy in filing

7. To overcome the manual collation problem, forms are frequently padded.
   Of the following statements which relate to this type of packaging, select the one that is MOST accurate.

   A. Typewritten forms which are prepared as padded forms are more efficient than all other packaging.
   B. Padded forms are best suited for handwritten forms.
   C. It is difficult for a printer to pad form copies of different colors.
   D. Registration problems increase when cut-sheet forms are padded.

8. Most forms are cut from a standard mill sheet of paper. This is the size on which forms dealers base their prices. Since an agency is paying for a full-size sheet of paper, it is the responsibility of the analyst to design forms so that as many as possible may be cut from the sheet without waste.
   Of the following sizes, select the one that will cut from a standard mill sheet with the GREATEST waste and should, therefore, be avoided if possible.

   A. 4" x 6"   B. 5" x 8"   C. 9" x 12"   D. $8\frac{1}{2}$" x 14"

9. Assume that the work in your department involves the use of many technical terms.
   In such a situation, when you are answering inquiries from the general public, it would usually be BEST to

   A. use simple language and avoid the technical terms
   B. use the technical terms whenever possible
   C. use technical terms freely, but explain each term in parentheses
   D. apologize if you are forced to use a technical term

10. You are answering a letter that was written on the letterhead of the ABC Company and signed by James H. Block, Treasurer.
    What is usually considered to be the CORRECT salutation to use in your reply?
    Dear

    A. ABC Company: B. Sirs:
    C. Mr. Block: D. Mr. Treasurer:

11. Assume that one of your duties is to handle routine letters of inquiry from the public. The one of the following which is usually considered to be MOST desirable in replying to such a letter is a

    A. detailed answer handwritten on the original letter of inquiry
    B. phone call since you can cover details more easily over the phone than in a letter
    C. short letter giving the specific information requested
    D. long letter discussing all possible aspects of the questions raised

12. The CHIEF reason for dividing a letter into paragraphs is to

    A. make the message clear to the reader by starting a new paragraph for each new topic
    B. make a short letter occupy as much of the page as possible
    C. keep the reader's attention by providing a pause from time to time
    D. make the letter look neat and businesslike

13. An *Attention* line is used in correspondence to

    A. indicate to the person receiving the correspondence that it contains an enclosure
    B. direct correspondence addressed to an organization to a particular individual within the organization
    C. greet the recipient of the correspondence
    D. highlight the main concern of the correspondence

14. In deciding upon the advisability of recording certain information on a regular basis, the MOST important consideration is:

    A. How much will it cost?
    B. Is it necessary?
    C. Is space available for keeping additional records?
    D. Will it fit into the work pattern?

15. Instructions for filling out simple forms should USUALLY appear

    A. at the bottom of the form
    B. on a separate sheet of instructions
    C. on the reverse side of the form
    D. with the items to which they refer

16. Each new form should be given a number PRIMARILY because

    A. it provides a means of easy reference
    B. names are not sufficiently descriptive
    C. numbering forms is common government practice
    D. numbers are more suitable for automatic data processing

17. Of the following, the MOST important features of an effective business letter are

    A. introduction and conclusion
    B. punctuation and paragraphing
    C. simplicity and clarity
    D. style and organization

18. When recording receipt of purchases of equipment, the one of the following which is usually LEAST important is

    A. identification of the item
    B. name of the vendor
    C. quantity of the item
    D. weight of the item

19. In deciding which data should be collected for permanent records, the MOST important consideration is the

    A. amount of data available
    B. ease of processing the different types of data
    C. type of record-keeping system involved
    D. use to which such data may be put

20. In a certain filing system, documents are consecutively numbered as they are filed, a register is maintained of such consecutively numbered documents, and a record is kept of the number of each document removed from the files and its destination.
    This system will NOT help in

    A. finding the present whereabouts of a particular document
    B. proving the accuracy of the data recorded on a certain document
    C. indicating whether observed existing documents were ever filed
    D. locating a desired document without knowing what its contents are

21. The inside address in a business letter indicates to whom the letter is to be sent.
    Of the following, the MOST important reason why a letter should contain the inside address is that the inside address

    A. gives the letter a personal, friendly tone
    B. simplifies the work of dictation and transcription
    C. gives the letter a balanced appearance
    D. identifies the addressee when the envelope containing the letter is discarded

22. The appearance of a business letter should make a favorable first impression on the person to whom the letter is sent.
    In order to make such an impression, it is LEAST important that the

    A. letter be centered on the page
    B. margins be as even as possible
    C. letter make a neat appearance
    D. paragraphs be of the same length

23. A typed rough draft of a report should be double-spaced and should have wide margins PRIMARILY in order to

    A. estimate the number of pages the report will contain
    B. allow space for making corrections in the report
    C. determine whether the report is well-organized
    D. make the report easy to read

24. Suppose that you are assigned to make a number of original typewritten copies of a printed report. In doing this assignment, you type the first copy from the printed report and then type each subsequent copy from the last one you prepared.
   You could be MOST certain that there were no errors made in the copies if you found no errors when comparing the

   A. printed report with any one of the copies
   B. first copy with the printed report
   C. last copy with the printed report
   D. first copy with the last copy

25. Before typing on more than one copy of a printed form, the one of the following which you should do FIRST is to

   A. align the type so that the tails of the longer letters will rest on the lines printed on the form
   B. check the alignment of the copies of the forms by holding them up to the light
   C. insert the carbon paper into the typewriter and then insert the copies of the form
   D. insert the copies of the form into the typewriter and then insert the carbon paper

KEY (CORRECT ANSWERS)

1.	B	11.	C
2.	D	12.	A
3.	A	13.	B
4.	B	14.	B
5.	D	15.	D
6.	D	16.	A
7.	B	17.	C
8.	C	18.	D
9.	A	19.	D
10.	C	20.	B

21.	D
22.	D
23.	B
24.	C
25.	B

TEST 3

DIRECTIONS: Each question or incomplete statement is followed by several suggested answers or completions. Select the one that BEST answers the question or completes the statement. *PRINT THE LETTER OF THE CORRECT ANSWER IN THE SPACE AT THE RIGHT.*

1. The supervisor who makes a special point of using long words in preparing written reports is, in general, PROBABLY being

   A. *unwise* because a written report should be factual and accurate
   B. *unwise* because simplicity in a report is usually desirable
   C. *wise* because the written report will become a permanent record
   D. *wise* because with long words he can use the right emphasis in his report

   1.____

2. Before you turn in a report you have written of an investigation that you made, you discover some additional information that you didn't know about before.
   Whether or not you rewrite your report to include this additional information should depend MAINLY on the

   A. amount of time left in which to submit the report
   B. effect this information will have on the conclusions of the report
   C. number of changes that you will have to make in your original report
   D. possibility of turning in a supplementary report later

   2.____

3. When an applicant is approved for public assistance, the supervising clerk must fill in standard forms with certain information.
   The GREATEST advantage of using standard forms in this situation rather than having the supervising clerk write the report as he sees fit is that

   A. the report can be acted on quickly
   B. the report can be written without directions from a supervisor
   C. needed information is less likely to be left out of the report
   D. information that is written up this way is more likely to be verified

   3.____

4. In some types of reports, visual aids add interest, meaning, and support. They also provide an essential means of effectively communicating the message of the report.
   Of the following, the selection of the suitable visual aids to use with a report is LEAST dependent on the

   A. nature and scope of the report
   B. way in which the aid is to be used
   C. aids used in other reports
   D. prospective readers of the report

   4.____

5. A report is often revised several times before final preparation and distribution in an effort to make certain the report meets the needs of the situation for which it is designed.
   Which of the following is the BEST way for the author to be sure that a report covers the areas he intended?

   A. Obtain a co-worker's opinion
   B. Compare it with a content checklist
   C. Test it on a subordinate
   D. Check his bibliography

   5.____

6. Visual aids used in a report may be placed either in the text material or in the appendix. Deciding where to put a chart, table, or any such aid should depend on the

    A. title of the report
    B. purpose of the visual aid
    C. title of the visual aid
    D. length of the report

7. In which of the following situations is an oral report PREFERABLE to a written report? When a(n)

    A. recommendation is being made for a future plan of action
    B. department head requests immediate information
    C. long-standing policy change is made
    D. analysis of complicated statistical data is involved

8. All of the following rules will aid in producing clarity in report writing EXCEPT:

    A. Give specific details or examples, if possible
    B. Keep related words close together in each sentence
    C. Present information in sequential order
    D. Put several thoughts or ideas in each paragraph

9. When preparing a long report on a study prepared for your superior, the one of the following which should usually come FIRST in your report is a(n)

    A. brief description of the working procedure followed in your study
    B. review of the background conditions leading to the study
    C. summary of your conclusions
    D. outline of suggested procedures for implementing the report

10. The MAIN function of a research report is usually to

    A. convince the reader of the adequacy of the research
    B. report as expeditiously as possible what was done, why it was done, the results, and the conclusions
    C. contribute to the body of scientific knowledge
    D. substantiate an a priori conclusion by presenting a set of persuasive quantitative data

11. Words in a sentence must be arranged properly to make sure that the intended meaning of the sentence is clear. The sentence below that does NOT make sense because a clause has been separated from the word on which its meaning depends is:

    A. To be a good writer, clarity is necessary.
    B. To be a good writer, you must write clearly.
    C. You must write clearly to be a good writer.
    D. Clarity is necessary to good writing.

12. The use of a graph to show statistical data in a report is SUPERIOR to a table because it

    A. emphasizes approximations
    B. emphasizes facts and relationships more dramatically
    C. presents data more accurately
    D. is easily understood by the average reader

13. Of the following, the degree of formality required of a written report prepared by a labor relations specialist is MOST likely to depend on the

    A. subject matter of the report
    B. frequency of its occurrence
    C. amount of time available for its preparation
    D. audience for whom the report is intended

14. Of the following, a DISTINGUISHING characteristic of a written report intended for the head of your agency as compared to a report prepared for a lower-echelon staff member is that the report for the agency should usually include

    A. considerably more detail, especially statistical data
    B. the essential details in an abbreviated form
    C. all available source material
    D. an annotated bibliography

15. Assume that you are asked to write a lengthy report for use by the administrator of your agency, the subject of which is *The Impact of Proposed New Data Processing Operations on Line Personnel* in your agency. You decide that the most appropriate type of report for you to prepare is an analytical report, including recommendations.
    The MAIN reason for your decision is that

    A. the subject of the report is extremely complex
    B. large sums of money are involved
    C. the report is being prepared for the administrator
    D. you intend to include charts and graphs

16. Assume that you are preparing a report based on a survey dealing with the attitudes of employees in Division X regarding proposed new changes in compensating employees for working overtime. Three percent of the respondents to the survey voluntarily offer an unfavorable opinion on the method of assigning overtime work, a question not specifically asked of the employees.
    On the basis of this information, the MOST appropriate and significant of the following comments for you to make in the report with regard to employees' attitudes on assigning overtime work is that

    A. an insignificant percentage of employees dislike the method of assigning overtime work
    B. three percent of the employees in Division X dislike the method of assigning overtime work
    C. three percent of the sample selected for the survey voiced an unfavorable opinion on the method of assigning overtime work
    D. some employees voluntarily voiced negative feelings about the method of assigning overtime work, making it impossible to determine the extent of this attitude

17. Four parts of a survey report are listed below, not necessarily in their proper order:
    I. Body of report
    II. Synopsis of report
    III. Letter of transmittal
    IV. Conclusions
    Which one of the following represents the BEST sequence for inclusion of these parts in a report?

    A. III, IV, I, II   B. II, I, III, IV   C. III, II, I, IV   D. I, III, IV, II

18. Of the following, the MOST important value of a good report is that it

    A. reflects credit upon the person who submitted the report
    B. provides good reference material
    C. expedites official business
    D. expresses the need for official action

19. The MOST important requirement in report writing is

    A. promptness in turning in reports
    B. length
    C. grammatical construction
    D. accuracy

20. You have discovered an error in your report submitted to the main office. You should

    A. wait until the error is discovered in the main office and then correct it
    B. go directly to the supervisor in the main office after working hours and ask him unofficially to correct the answer
    C. notify the main office immediately so that the error can be corrected if necessary
    D. do nothing since it is possible that one error will have little effect on the total report

21. When you determine the methods of emphasis you will use in typing the titles, headings, and subheadings of a report, the one of the following which it is MOST important to keep in mind is that

    A. all headings of the same rank should be typed in the same way
    B. all headings should be typed in the single style which is most pleasing to the eye
    C. headings should not take up more than one-third of the page width
    D. only one method should be used for all headings, whatever their rank

22. Proper division of a letter into paragraphs requires that the writer of business letters should, as much as possible, be sure that

    A. each paragraph is short
    B. each paragraph develops discussion of just one topic
    C. each paragraph repeats the theme of the total message
    D. there are at least two paragraphs for every message

23. An editor is given a letter with this initial paragraph:
    We have received your letter, which we read with interest, and we are happy to respond to your question. In fact, we talked with several people in our office to get ideas to send to you.
    Which of the following is it MOST reasonable for the editor to conclude?
    The paragraph is

    A. concise
    B. communicating something of value
    C. unnecessary
    D. coherent

24. In preparing a report that includes several tables, if not otherwise instructed, the typist should MOST properly include a list of tables

    A. in the introductory part of the report
    B. at the end of each chapter in the body of the report
    C. in the supplementary part of the report as an appendix
    D. in the supplementary part of the report as a part of the index

25. You have been asked to write a report on methods of hiring and training new employees. Your report is going to be about ten pages long.
    For the convenience of your readers, a brief summary of your findings should

    A. appear at the beginning of your report
    B. be appended to the report as a postscript
    C. be circulated in a separate memo
    D. be inserted in tabular form in the middle of your report

26. A new student program is being set up for which certain new forms will be needed. You have been asked to design these forms.
    Of the following, the FIRST step you should take in planning the forms is

    A. finding out the exact purpose for which each form will be used
    B. deciding what size of paper should be used for each form
    C. determining whether multiple copies will be needed for any of the forms
    D. setting up a new filing system to handle the new forms

27. Many government agencies require the approval by a central forms control unit of the design and reproduction of new office forms.
    The one of the following results of this procedure that is a DISADVANTAGE is that requiring prior approval of a central forms control unit usually

    A. limits the distribution of forms to those offices with justifiable reasons for receiving them
    B. permits checking whether existing forms or modifications of them are in line with current agency needs
    C. encourages reliance on only the central office to set up all additional forms when needed
    D. provides for someone with a specialized knowledge of forms design to review and criticize new and revised forms

28. Suppose that you are assigned to prepare a form from which certain information will be posted in a ledger.
    It would be MOST helpful to the person posting the information in the ledger if, in designing the form, you were to

    A. use the same color paper for both the form and the ledger
    B. make the form the same size as the pages of the ledger
    C. have the information on the form in the same order as that used in the ledger
    D. include in the form a box which is to be initialed when the data on the form have been posted in the ledger

29. In the effective design of office forms, the FIRST step to take is to

   A. decide what information should be included
   B. decide the purpose for which the form will be used
   C. identify the form by name and number
   D. identify the employees who will be using the form

30. Some designers of office forms prefer to locate the instructions on how to fill out the form at the bottom of it.
    The MOST logical objection to placing such instructions at the bottom of the form is that

   A. instructions at the bottom require an excess of space
   B. all form instructions should be outlined with a separate paragraph
   C. the form may be partly filled out before the instructions are seen
   D. the bottom of the form should be reserved only for authorization and signature

KEY (CORRECT ANSWERS)

1.	B	11.	A	21.	A		
2.	B	12.	B	22.	B		
3.	C	13.	D	23.	C		
4.	C	14.	B	24.	A		
5.	B	15.	A	25.	A		
6.	B	16.	D	26.	A		
7.	B	17.	C	27.	C		
8.	D	18.	C	28.	C		
9.	C	19.	D	29.	B		
10.	B	20.	C	30.	C		

CAREERS IN THERAPY

CONTENTS

	Page
Location of Positions to be Filled	1
Description of Work	1
Physical Therapist Positions-Grades GS6-9	1
Occupational Therapist Positions-Grades GS6-9	1
Corrective Therapist Positions-Grades GS6-9	2
Educational Therapist Positions-Grades GS5-9	2
Manual Arts Therapist Positions-Grades GS5-9	2
Requirements	2
Corrective Therapist	2
Education	2
Experience	3
Qualifying Experience	3
Substitution of Education for Experience	3
Educational Therapist	4
Education	4
Experience	4
Qualifying Experience	4
Substitution of Education for Experience	5
Manual Arts Therapist	5
Education	5
Experience	5
Qualifying Experience	6
Substitution of Education for Experience	6
Occupational Therapist	6
Education	6
Foreign Schools	7
Experience	7
Substitution of Education for Experience	7
Physical Therapist	8
Education	8
Experience	8
Substitution of Education for Experience	9
Information Concerning All Positions	9
Quality Graduate	9
Unpaid Experience or Volunteer Work	10
Quality Experience	10
Equal Employment Opportunity	10
General Information	10
How to Apply	11
Where to Obtain Forms	11

CAREERS IN THERAPY

The Federal service offers purposeful and interesting careers to trained therapists who are seeking active participation in programs dedicated to the treatment of sick or disabled patients. Excellent opportunities are provided for persons with such training to contribute through prescribed activities to the recovery of patients and to enable them to achieve a greater degree of independence. Persons appointed will become active participants in programs which include patient care and treatment, administrative responsibilities, research studies, and the opportunity to acquire additional training.

LOCATION OF POSITIONS TO BE FILLED

The positions to be filled from this examination are located in Washington, D.C., and throughout the United States. The principal using agencies are:

The Veterans Administration which plans to fill Therapist positions in all specialties throughout the United States and Puerto Rico, and

The U.S. Public Health Service which plans to fill Occupational and Physical Therapist positions throughout the United States.

In addition, a limited number of positions in the District of Columbia Government and in other Federal agencies throughout the United States and in foreign countries will be filled from this examination.

DESCRIPTION OF WORK

Physical Therapist Positions -- Grades GS6 through GS9

Physical Therapists perform and interpret tests and measures of neurological and neuromuscular skeletal functions as an aid to treatment; plan the initial and subsequent treatment programs on the basis of these test findings as directed by the referring physician; and administer treatment through the use of therapeutic exercises, massage, mechanical devices and therapeutic agents which employ the physical, chemical and other properties of air, water, electricity, sound and radiant energy.

Occupational Therapist Positions -- Grades GS6 through GS9

Occupational Therapists plan, administer, and supervise medically prescribed occupational therapy treatments to patients by the scientific use of remedial activities such as machine and hand crafts properly selected and adapted to assist in promoting physical, mental, and social well-being; and in providing restoration of muscle function and joint motion, improved work tolerance, and motivation back to normal life as a useful member of society.

Corrective Therapist Positions -- Grades GS6 through GS9
Corrective Therapists plan and administer medically prescribed physical exercise directed toward maintaining or improving the general state of health of patients by preventing muscular deterioration, conserving and increasing strength, and restoring function. They guide patients in ambulation and develop proficiency in the routine of personal hygiene for bedfast patients.

Educational Therapist Positions -- Grades GS5 through GS9
Educational Therapists plan and administer medically prescribed instruction in courses and related activities of a medical evaluative and treatment nature in a comprehensive educational therapy program. They utilize a large variety of courses and rehabilitation activities in one or more of the following areas: academic, commercial fine arts, science, and general.

Manual Arts Therapist Positions -- Grades GS5 through GS9
Manual Arts Therapists plan and administer medically prescribed treatment of an evaluative nature in a comprehensive manual arts therapy program. They utilize a variety of combinations of specialized areas which have a vocational significance in the rehabilitation of the patient; for example, metalworking, woodworking, electricity, graphic and applied arts, agriculture, industrial therapy, and general.

REQUIREMENTS
  Special Notice to Students
  Applications will be accepted from students who are within 9 months of completing the courses set forth below in the educational requirements for each position. Such students who are qualified in all other respects may receive provisional appointments but may not enter on duty until they submit proof of completion of the required courses.

CORRECTIVE THERAPIST

Education
Applicants for all grades must have completed the requirements for a bachelor's degree from an accredited college or university with a major in physical education. In addition, this education must have included or been supplemented by clinical practice that consisted of at least 240 clock hours. This clinical practice must have been obtained in a Veterans Administration clinical training program or an equivalent training program in a clinical setting under the direction of a physician. It must have been developed with an accredited college or university which offers a major in physical education in conjunction with a hospital or rehabilitation center.

Experience

In addition to the educational requirements, applicants must meet experience requirements as follows:

GS6 -- None

GS7 -- Six months of professional experience which shows a full professional understanding of the theories of treatment by corrective therapy and their proper application through the use of corrective and therapeutic physical rehabilitation and reconditioning procedures.

GS8 -- In addition to the requirements for the GS7 level, 6 months of professional experience. At least 6 months of the total experience must have been in a clinical program involving work from medical prescriptions and participation with physicians in the development of treatment plans and evaluation of procedures.

GS9 -- In addition to the requirements for the GS8 level, 6 months of experience which demonstrates a broad knowledge and understanding of the principles and techniques in the use of corrective therapy. This experience must include interpretation of physicians' prescriptions, modification of standard techniques in unusual cases, and programming for patients. For positions which include the responsibility for conducting a special program, such as spinal cord injury, psychiatric, hemiplegic, chronic lung disease, cardiorespiratory evaluation and conditioning or clinical training, applicants must show 6 months of specialized experience or training in such a program.

Qualifying Experience

Qualifying experience must have been in a program of corrective and therapeutic physical rehabilitation or reconditioning in a hospital, domiciliary, convalescent or nursing home, rehabilitation center, school or private office of a physician, or other organized treatment program which was medically directed.

Substitution of Education for Experience

GS7 -- A master's degree from an accredited college or university in a field appropriate to corrective therapy, such as physical education with substantial study in subjects such as anatomy, physiology or kinesiology, and the clinical practice will meet all of the requirements for the GS7 level.

GS9 -- Successful completion of 2 years of graduate study in the above fields and the clinical practice will meet all of the requirements for the GS9 level.

EDUCATIONAL THERAPIST

Education

Applicants for all grades must have completed all of the requirements for a bachelor's degree from an accredited college or university with a major appropriate to one of the following areas: academic, commercial, fine arts, or science, including or supplemented by at least 12 semester hours in the field of education.

Experience

In addition to the educational requirements, applicants meet experience requirements as follows:

GS5 -- None

GS6 -- Six months of professional educational therapy experience.

GS7 -- In addition to the requirements for the GS6 level, 6 months of professional experience which shows a full professional understanding of the theories of treatment by educational therapy and their proper application and knowledge of pertinent subject-matter fields.

GS8 -- In addition to the requirements for the GS7 level, 6 months of professional experience. At least 6 months of the total experience must have been in a clinical program involving work from medical prescriptions and participation with physicians in the development of treatment plans and evaluation of procedures.

GS9 -- In addition to the requirements for the GS8 level, 6 months of professional experience which demonstrates a broad knowledge and understanding of the principles and techniques in the use of educational therapy. This experience must include interpretation of physicians' prescriptions, modification of standard techniques in unusual cases and programming for patients. For positions which include the responsibility for conducting a special program, such as spinal cord injury, psychiatric, day care, chronic lung disease, clinical training, or language retraining, applicants must show 6 months of specialized experience or training in such a program.

Qualifying Experience

Such experience must have been acquired in an educational or educational therapy program of rehabilitation or reconditioning in a hospital, rehabilitation center, sheltered workshop, school for the handicapped, homebound educational program, or other organized treatment program which was medically directed.

Substitution of Education For Experience

GS6 -- Sucessful completion of a program of clinical practice in educational therapy consisting of at least 240 clock hours may be substituted for 6 months of the required professional experience. This clinical practice must have been obtained in a VA clinical training program or an equivalent training program in a clinical setting under the direction of a physician. The program must have been developed with an accredited college or university in conjunction with a hospital or rehabilitation center.

GS7 -- Successful completion of all the requirements for the master's degree from an accredited college or university in education, or in a field appropriate to the specialization of the particular position and the clinical practice will meet the experience requirements for the grade GS7.

GS9 -- Successful completion of 2 years of graduate studies in the above field and the clinical practice will meet the experience requirements for the grade GS9.

MANUAL ARTS THERAPIST

Education

Applicants for all grades must have completed all of the requirements for a bachelor's degree from an accredited college or university with a major in industrial arts teacher education, industrial education, agriculture, or manual arts therapy.

Experience

In addition to the educational requirements, applicants must meet experience requirements as follows:

GS5 -- None

GS6 -- Six months of professional manual arts therapy experience.

GS7 -- In addition to the requirements for the GS6 level, 6 months of professional experience which shows that the applicant possesses a full professional understanding of the theories of treatment by manual arts therapy and their proper application and knowledge of the specializations applicable to the particular positions to be filled.

GS8 -- In addition to the requirements for the GS7 level, 6 months of professional experience. At least 6 months of the total experience must have been in a clinical program involving work from medical prescriptions and participation with physicians in the development of treatment plans and evaluation of procedures.

GS9 -- In addition to the requirements for the GS8 level, 6 months of experience which demonstrates a broad knowledge and understanding of the principles and techniques in the use of manual arts therapy. This experience must include interpretation of physicians' prescriptions, modification of standard techniques in unusual cases and programming for patients. For positions that include the responsibility for conducting a special program, such as spinal cord injury, psychiatric, geriatric, day care, chronic lung disease, clinic training, community hospital industrial rehabilitation programs, applicants must show 6 months of specialized experience or training in such a program.

Qualifying Experience
Such experience must have been in a manual arts therapy program of rehabilitation or reconditioning in a hospital rehabilitation, center, sheltered workshop, school for the handicapped or other organized treatment program which was medically directed.

Substitution of Education For Experience
GS6 -- Sucessful completion of a program of clinical practice in manual arts therapy of at least 240 clock hours fully meets the requirements for the GS6 level. This clinical practice must have been obtained in a Veterans Administration clinical training program or an equivalent training program in a clinical setting under the direction of a physician. The program must have been developed with an accredited college or university in conjunction with a hospital or rehabilitation center.
GS7 -- A master's degree from an accredited college or university in manual arts therapy, industrial arts teacher education, industrial education, or agriculture, and the clinical practice will meet the experience requirements for the grade GS7.
GS9 -- The successful completion of 2 years of graduate study in the above fields and the clinical practice will meet the requirements for the grade GS9.

OCCUPATIONAL THERAPIST

Education
Applicants for all grades must have completed a curriculum in occupational therapy approved at the time of their graduation by the Council of Medical Education and Hospitals of the American Medical Association. Applicants who graduated prior to 1938 must be graduates of schools or courses approved at the time of their graduation by the American Occupational Therapy Association. Further, applicants must have successfully completed the clinical affiliation requirements prescribed by the degree-awarding school.

Foreign Schools

Graduates of foreign schools of occupational therapy will meet the above qualifications if they have successfully completed all requirements of a curriculum of occupational therapy approved by a member association of the World Federation of Occupational Therapists.

Experience

In addition to the educational requirements, applicants must meet experience requirements as follows:

GS6 -- None

GS7 -- Six months of professional experience as an occupational therapist under medical supervision in a hospital, sanitarium, rehabilitation center, community health program, or clinic. This experience must show that the applicant possesses a full professional understanding of the theories of treatment by occupational therapy and their proper application through the use of activities utilizing skills such as are involved in woodworking, printing, arts and crafts, etc.

GS8 -- In addition to the requirements for the GS7 level, 6 months of professional experience which has demonstrated the ability to work independently, devising treatment for patients with the normal range of problems.

GS9 -- In addition to the requirements for the GS8 level, 6 months of professional experience which demonstrates a broad knowledge and understanding of the principles and techniques in the use of occupational therapy treatment for patients. This experience must show that the applicant possesses the ability to interpret physicians' prescriptions for occupational therapy treatment, that he can modify standard techniques in unusual cases, and program for patients.

Substitution of Education for Experience

GS7 -- The successful completion of all of the requirements for the master's degree from an accredited college or university in a field appropriate to occupational therapy (such as anatomy, kinesiology, or mental hygiene) will meet the experience requirements for the grade GS7.

GS9 -- The successful completion of 2 years of graduate study in such fields as the above or in education, social psychology, or physiology, will meet the experience requirements for the grade GS9.

PHYSICAL THERAPIST

Education

Applicants for all grades must be graduates of physical therapy curriculums approved by the American Physical Therapy Association from 1928 to 1936; or by the Council on Medical Education and Hospitals of the American Medical Association from 1936 to 1960; or by the Council on Medical Education and Hospitals of the American Medical Association in collaboration with the American Pyysical Therapy Association since 1960. Further, applicants must have successfully completed the clinical-affiliation requirements prescribed by the degree-awarding school; OR

A physical therapist trained outside the United States shall

1. Be a graduate since 1928 from a physical therapy curriculum approved in the country in which the curriculum was located. The curriculum must be in a country in which there is a member organization of the World Confederation for Physical Therapy.
2. Complete successfully a qualifying examination as prescribed by the American Physical Therapy Association.

Experience

In addition to the educational requirements, applicants must meet experience requirements as follows:

GS6 -- None

GS7 -- Six months of professional experience as a physical therapist under medical supervision, in a hospital, sanitarium, orthopedic clinic, rehabilitation center, community health program; in an outpatient clinic, industry, school of physical therapy, school of special education, or in the office of a licensed doctor of medicine. The experience must show that the applicant possesses a full professional understanding of the theories of treatment by physical therapy, and their proper applications.

GS8 -- In addition to the requirements for the GS7 level, 6 months of professional experience, which has demonstrated the ability to work independently, devising treatment for patients with the normal range of problems.

GS9 -- In addition to the requirements for the GS8 level, 6 months of professional experience which demonstrates a broad knowledge and understanding of the principles and procedures in the use of physical therapy treatment for patients. This experience must show that the applicant possesses the ability to interpet physicians' prescriptions for physical therapy treatment, that he can modify standard techniques in unusual cases, and program for patients.

Substitution of Education for Experience

GS7 -- The successful completion of all of the requirements for the master's degree in a field appropriate to physical therapy will be accepted as meeting the full requirement for the grade GS7.

GS9 -- The successful completion of 2 years of graduate study in such fields as behavioral kinesiology, anatomy, physiology, psychology, or physical education, with concentration of study related to physical therapy, will meet the experience requirements for the grade GS9.

INFORMATION CONCERNING ALL POSITIONS

Quality Graduate

Persons who have completed within the last 2 years all the requirements for or are candidates for the bachelor's degree from an accredited college or university within 9 months (with appropriate majors or course credits, if required) may be rated eligible for GS7 provided they have completed the clinical practice and they meet one of the requirements listed below.

    a. Standing in the upper 25 percent of their class based on completed college work at the time of application for the position. This is the upper quarter of the class in the college or university, or major subdivision (e.g., school of therapy, school of education).

    b. College grade average of "B" (3.0) or better (or equivalent). This is either
       (1) the average of all completed college courses at the time of application for the position, OR
       (2) the average of all college courses completed during the last 2 years of the undergraduate curriculum.

    c. College grade average of B+ (3.5) or better (or equivalent) in their major field, where such field is fully qualifying and directly applicable to the specialty field of the position to be filled. This is either
       (1) the average of completed courses in the major field at the time of application for the position, OR
       (2) the average of college courses completed in the major field during the last 2 years of the undergraduate curriculum.

    d. Election to membership in Phi Beta Kappa, Sigma Xi, or one of the national honorary scholastic societies meeting the minimum requirements of the Association of College Honor Societies, other than freshman honor societies.

e. A score of 600 or better on an Area Test or an Advanced Test of the Graduate Record Examination. (Senior students may be rated provisionally eligible under b(2) or c(2) above, provided they had the required average in the junior year. They will be required to submit evidence at the time of appointment that the required average was maintained during the senior year.)

Unpaid Experience or Volunteer Work

Credit will be given for unpaid experience or volunteer work such as in community, cultural, social service, and professional association activities, on the same basis as for paid experience; that is, it must be of the type acceptable under this announcement. Therefore, applicants may, if they wish, report such experience in one or more of the experience blocks at the end of their employment history if they feel that it represents qualifying experience for the position for which they are applying. To receive proper credit applicants must show the actual time, such as the number of hours a week, spent in such activity.

Quality of Experience

The number of years of experience required for any grade level represents the minimum amount of time necessary to qualify for the positions but length of time alone is not of itself qualifying. The applicant's work experience must also have been of a quality and scope sufficient to enable him to perform satisfactorily assignments typical of the grade level for which he is being considered. Applicants for positions at GS9 and below (except those qualifying solely on the basis of education) must have had 6 months of experience at a level equivalent to the next lower grade in the Federal Service or 1 year equivalent to the second lower grade.

Equal Employment Opportunity

All qualified applicants will receive consideration for appointment without regard to race, religion, color, national origin, or sex.

General Information

For information about citizenship, physical requirements, age, kinds of appointments, veterans preference and other general information, see Civil Service Commission Pamphlet No. 4, "Working for the U.S.A.," which may be obtained at most places where applications are available.

HOW TO APPLY
  What to File
    1. SF-57
        Please show the title of the position for which you are applying, the announcement number, and the lowest salary you are willing to accept. Be sure to include your Zip Code as part of your address.
    2. Card Form 5001-ABC.
    3. Supplementary Information Sheet
        For all positions, please use the Supplementary Information Sheet to indicate your major field of college study, and when and where you have completed an advanced program of clinical practice. In addition, show the length of time in clock hours spent in the program of clinical practice, and any specialized therapy experience you may have had.
    4. CSC Form 226
        If you wish to qualify for the grade GS7 on the basis of being a *quality graduate*, you should complete and submit with your application the CSC Form 226 (Part II only).
        If you are a graduate student, you may use the Form 226, Part I, or the Supplementary Information Sheet to show the courses and semester-hour credits you expect to complete within the subsequent 9 months. Transcripts of college records may be used whenever appropriate, if you prefer.
    5. SF-15
        SF-15, with documentary proof required therein, if you are claiming 10-point preference (disability, widow, wife, or mother preference). Documentary evidence will be returned to applicants.

WHERE TO OBTAIN FORMS
  The forms mentioned above may be obtained from
    (1) Job Information Centers in many large cities (their addresses are listed in pages 22 through 30 in Pamphlet 4),
    (2) many post offices except in cities where the Job Information Centers are located, or
    (3) the Interagency Board at the address below.

WHERE AND WHEN TO FILE
  Send applications to the address shown below. Applications will be accepted when an official Announcement has been issued advertising these positions.

>   Interagency Board of U.S. Civil Service
>   Examiners for Washington, D.C.
>   1900 E Street NW
>   Washington, D.C. 20415

BASIC FUNDAMENTALS OF
Rehabilitation Nursing Care
Contents

Page

SECTION I:

BASIC PHILOSOPHY AND PRINCIPLES OF REHABILITATION NURSING

Principles of Rehabilitation for Nursing Homes	1
Nursing Home Team	3
Rehabilitation Nursing	7
Relationship of the Activities and the Rehabilitation Nursing Areas	9

SECTION II:

PRINCIPLES AND TECHNIQUES OF REHABILITATION NURSING PROCEDURES

Body Alignment	13
Introduction to Exercises	19
Normal Body Motions	21
Passive Range of Motion Exercises	33
Transfer Activities	39
Ambulation Activities	45
Activities of Daily Living	59
Skin Care	67
Personal Hygiene	68
Bowel and Bladder Training	71

Section I

Basic Philosophy and Principles of Rehabilitation Nursing

Principles of Rehabilitation for Nursing Homes

Rehabilitation means a variety of things to many people. For purposes of this manual, rehabilitation means the care given to chronically ill, disabled, and aged patients in nursing homes to help them do more for themselves and become less dependent upon others.

BASIC PRINCIPLES

- See the patient as a *whole* person.
- Stress the patient's abilities.
- Keep the patient active.
- Start treatment early.

DISCUSSION OF PRINCIPLES

See the patient as a whole person. Seeing the patient as a *whole* person means understanding him as an individual, as a member of his family and of the community. No two individuals are exactly alike; each has his own likes and dislikes, and his own wants and fears. The kind of person who can help patients in a nursing home is one who likes older people, understands their demands, senses their needs, and is tolerant of their slowness and forgetfulness. Kindness and patience with understanding will save nursing personnel from making the frequent mistake of treating the older patient like a child. To have the patient's cooperation, the nursing staff must show him that he is still important and give him a feeling of security by letting him know someone cares. If the nursing personnel honestly care, the patient will be the first to recognize it. When they offer him hope and help him accept and live with his physical condition, they encourage him to become less dependent. Their concern should be not only with the illness of the patient, but about the person who is the patient.

Stress the patient's abilities. It is easy to recognize what the patient *cannot* do for himself. Part of the rehabilitation procedure is to recognize the things the patient *can* do without help. It is important to emphasize the things the patient can do rather than those he cannot do; to show the patient how to do things for himself that he has not done for a long time. As nursing personnel gain experience with rehabilitation techniques, they will find it easier to teach or remind the patient that he *can* still do many things and is a valuable member of his family, his social group and the community.

Keep the patient active. The fact that activity strengthens and inactivity wastes is of prime importance. When the patient uses his own muscles, he becomes stronger and can begin to assume more responsibility for his own care and activities. As the patient does more for himself, he makes use of his mind as well as his body. He becomes more alert and more interested in the people around him and in his activities. There may be times when a patient is unable to exercise himself; it is then that exercises must be done for him with the nurse's help. Planned exercises will help improve the patient's strength and encourage him to try new steps each day toward independent living. Just knowing that something is being done for him and that someone is interested enough to do it does much to give him new hope.

Start treatment early. It is extremely important that rehabilitation procedures be established early in the patient's illness. Because it offers immediate hope, early treatment does not allow the patient to become mentally depressed and discouraged. Early treatment in rehabilitation helps prevent disabling conditions and prolonged bed rest. Early treatment also has more lasting results. The patient must be encouraged to do things for himself and to have a variety of interests. He is happiest when he is learning to do for himself and working toward the day when he is again self-sufficient.

Nursing Home Team

The team approach in caring for a patient means simply that there must be teamwork between the patient and everyone who is interested in him. Everyone must be working in the same direction, at the same time, for the same results. As the chart on page 5 shows, the nursing home team has six members: the patient, his physician, the nursing staff, the activities director, the community, and the patient's family.

PATIENT

The patient is always the center of the team's attention. The team approach is used to offer every possible resource in helping the patient to help himself. For the patient to benefit from rehabilitation, all of the team members, including the patient, must work together.

PATIENT'S PHYSICIAN

The team's direction regarding the treatment and care of the patient comes from the patient's physician. He knows the physical condition of the patient and uses this knowledge to guide the other team members regarding the rehabilitation program for his patient.

NURSING STAFF

The nursing staff takes its orders from the patient's physician and is responsible for seeing that the patient receives the necessary nursing care. In rehabilitative nursing, the nurse does the teaching of the patient to help him regain the highest degree of independence possible.

ACTIVITIES DIRECTOR

The activities director of the nursing home is responsible for that part of the rehabilitation program which includes crafts, recreation, and the organization and coordination of volunteer programs. These activities must be useful and purposeful, *never* just busy work. Activities carefully selected to use old skills and develop new ones encourage the patient to be more active and independent. The activities director works through the nursing personnel and physicians in planning the activity program.

COMMUNITY

The nursing home patient is a member of the community and needs to feel that he is still *part* of that community. This may be achieved by the patient's going to church services in the community, to the polls to vote, to the public library, and to various other community functions. The nursing home should maintain and use a list of resource agencies to aid in meeting specific problems of both the patient and the home. The interest of the community in the nursing home may be aroused by periodically holding an "open house," holding religious services, and utilizing volunteer groups.

FAMILY

The family's attitudes, interests, and desires have an important and direct influence on how the patient responds to treatment. It is important to keep the family informed of the "what and why" of the patient's rehabilitation program, to show them how they may participate in the program, and to keep them posted on the patient's progress. This will be effective in promoting good family-patient relationships, good nurse-family relationships, and good nursing home-community relationships.

Nursing Home Team

Rehabilitation Nursing

In rehabilitation nursing, the nurse assists the patient to do for himself rather than doing everything for the patient. This concept is difficult for many nurses to accept and apply. If self-care is to be achieved the nurse must remember to use the patient's abilities no matter how limited they may be, and to accept the idea that the older patient can be rehabilitated for independent living.

NURSING OBJECTIVES

- To understand the patient as a person who is still a member of his family and community.
- To understand the personality changes that result from aging, long-term illness and disability, and that influence the patient to not care whether he is able to do for himself again.
- To recognize the need of counsel and guidance for the patient and his family in helping them meet their social, economic, recreational, and vocational problems through referrals to appropriate community resources.
- To know and apply good general nursing care as determined by the physician and the individual patient's needs; for example, nutrition, skin care, oral hygiene, elimination, exercise and rest.
- To understand and use certain rehabilitative nursing techniques such as —
    Range of motion exercises to maintain movement.
    Self-care, transfer, and walking activities.
    Bowel and bladder training.
    Good positioning to maintain body alignment.
- To remember that the nurse is an important part of the patient's life and can help influence him by her attitudes and actions.

SPECIAL EQUIPMENT

At times there is need to use special equipment that may assist in the patient's rehabilitation. Nurses on all shifts should understand how to use braces, crutches, parallel bars, and pulleys and know the purpose of devices made for patients to help feed or dress themselves. The patient needs encouragement and understanding in learning how to use this equipment. Many times he is frightened or discouraged to the point of choosing to stay in bed rather than to get up only to struggle with an unfamiliar procedure.

8

APPROACH AND MOTIVATION

What is *approach?* What is *motivation?* Why are they important? Approach is to *draw near*. Motivation is that within a person rather than without that *moves* him to *action*.

It is important in the practice of rehabilitation to approach the patient in the right manner in order to motivate him to be rehabilitated. Motivating the older person may be difficult to do. To make him want to walk again, to wash himself, to dress himself is a task that takes patience, understanding, and gentle but firm persuasion on the part of the nurse. Each patient is handled differently; an approach that works with one may not work with another.

Usually, the older patient has lost the desire to do more for himself. In this situation the nurse needs to make the patient feel he is still worthwhile and can be useful. She must be realistic, however, and not expect the older patient to do that which he is not capable of doing. She should start with a simple task such as having him wash his face, and should give him support, if only to stand by and encourage him. The older patient needs instruction in doing even very simple things. He may have forgotten how or may believe he cannot do as well as he should in performing everyday tasks.

Some patients will not want to help themselves because they fear they will receive less attention from the nurse if they become too self-sufficient. Motivating the patient to learn any one independent activity will probably not be accomplished with the first attempt. It is essential to return to the patient *consistently* every day, encouraging him to do the same task again or beginning to work with him on a new one. He should not be ignored for he may feel the nurse does not want to be bothered with him or that he has been unsuccessful in his past effort to learn.

Approaching the patient with enthusiasm is very important, but he should not be overwhelmed with it. The nurse's "mood" is often the factor that encourages or discourages him. The patient may have a good potential for being motivated, but to develop that potential he must be surrounded by interested people who will stimulate him and understand him.

Relationship of the Activities and the Rehabilitation Nursing Areas

The nursing and the activities programs are each a part of rehabilitation. They should be closely related and coordinated. In many ways each area helps the other; each is a part of patient care.

RESPONSIBILITIES OF STAFF IN BOTH AREAS

- The staff should exchange information regarding the patient's feelings, his cooperation, what he is doing, his problems, and the staff's ideas for improving the program for the patient.
- Everyone should help the patient see that he can still do things he thought he could no longer do.
- Each staff person should reinforce the other's work with the patient — should show interest and enthusiasm; should encourage the patient to participate in both rehabilitation nursing and activities.

The staff can accomplish this by —

- Talking to the patient about what he is doing, his activities of daily living, about coming events or whatever is pertinent in either area.
- Attending the activity program.
- Participating in social activities for patients and staff as often as possible.
- Helping the patient want to be less dependent. It may be difficult for the nurse to interest the patient in his daily care. The nurse, as well as others, may remind the patient that there is something special planned for him today—something for him to do or make that he will enjoy—necessitating the completion of his daily care.

Everyone should plan cooperatively and should change schedules as necessary to provide the maximum services and opportunities for the patient. Other departments — food service, housekeeping, etc.—have much to offer and should be included in the planning.

ACTIVITIES DIRECTOR'S RESPONSIBILITIES

The activities director is responsible for —

• Planning, scheduling, and carrying out a varied program (individual and group activities) that will encourage patients to participate.

• Planning and conducting activities at times when they do not conflict or interfere with basic and rehabilitative nursing care as well as other necessary procedures of the nursing home—cleaning, meals, etc.

• Planning and conducting activities that will use the abilities and encourage the participation of the nursing home staff. Participation will promote a feeling of helpfulness on the part of the staff. The staff's enjoyment of participation in the activities will certainly be recognized by and carried over to the patients.

NURSING STAFF RESPONSIBILITIES

The activities director needs help in —

• Getting patients ready and to the area for activities. The nursing personnel should have patients ready at a specific time and help transport them to a specified area when the activities director has planned a group project.

• Developing new ideas for activities. The nursing personnel who are with the patients most often hear them comment on their likes and dislikes. Those remarks, if passed on to the activities director, can be useful in developing a more interesting program.

• Obtaining craft materials. Everyone can participate by telling relatives, friends, and organizations about the nursing home's activities program—its need for usable material such as nylon hose, scraps of cloth, yarn, wood, plastic, etc.

• Obtaining volunteers. If friends in the neighborhood, church organizations or other groups in the community learn of the need for volunteers in the nursing home, they may want to help with the program.

Section II

Principles and Techniques of Rehabilitation Nursing Procedures

Body Alignment

GOOD BODY ALIGNMENT AND BED POSITIONING

It is important that the patient who has to remain in bed for any length of time be kept comfortable. The patient should be positioned so that he is relaxed, arms and legs slightly bent (flexed), and is lying either on his side, back, or stomach. However, the hips and knees should not remain in the flexed position at all times as this promotes the development of contractures. When the patient is in either supine or prone position, the hips and knees should be extended as far as possible for at least part of the time.

It is essential that the patient's position be changed to prevent fatigue, contractures, and continuous pressure on any one part of the body. The patient's position should be changed *at least every 2 hours, day and night*. The patient should be taught how to assist in changing his position and, when possible, to do this independently.

A firm mattress and springs are essential for maintaining good body alignment. A bedboard may be placed between the mattress and springs to prevent the mattress from sagging with the weight of the body. A footboard may be used to position the patient's feet at right angles to the legs in the supine and prone positions. A footboard also eliminates the danger of bedding drawing tightly over the patient's feet.

Tight bedding, especially for the weak and debilitated patient who remains unmoving in bed most of the time, can cause discomfort and further reduction of movement. Sheets tucked in tightly over the patient's toes and feet may cause foot deformities and ingrown toenails. Under tight bedding, the foot is held in plantar flexion, allowing tightening of the heel cord. The resulting inability to place the heel on the floor when attempting to stand or walk creates a painful stretch and makes walking difficult, if not impossible.

Good Body Alignment and Bed Positioning—*continued*

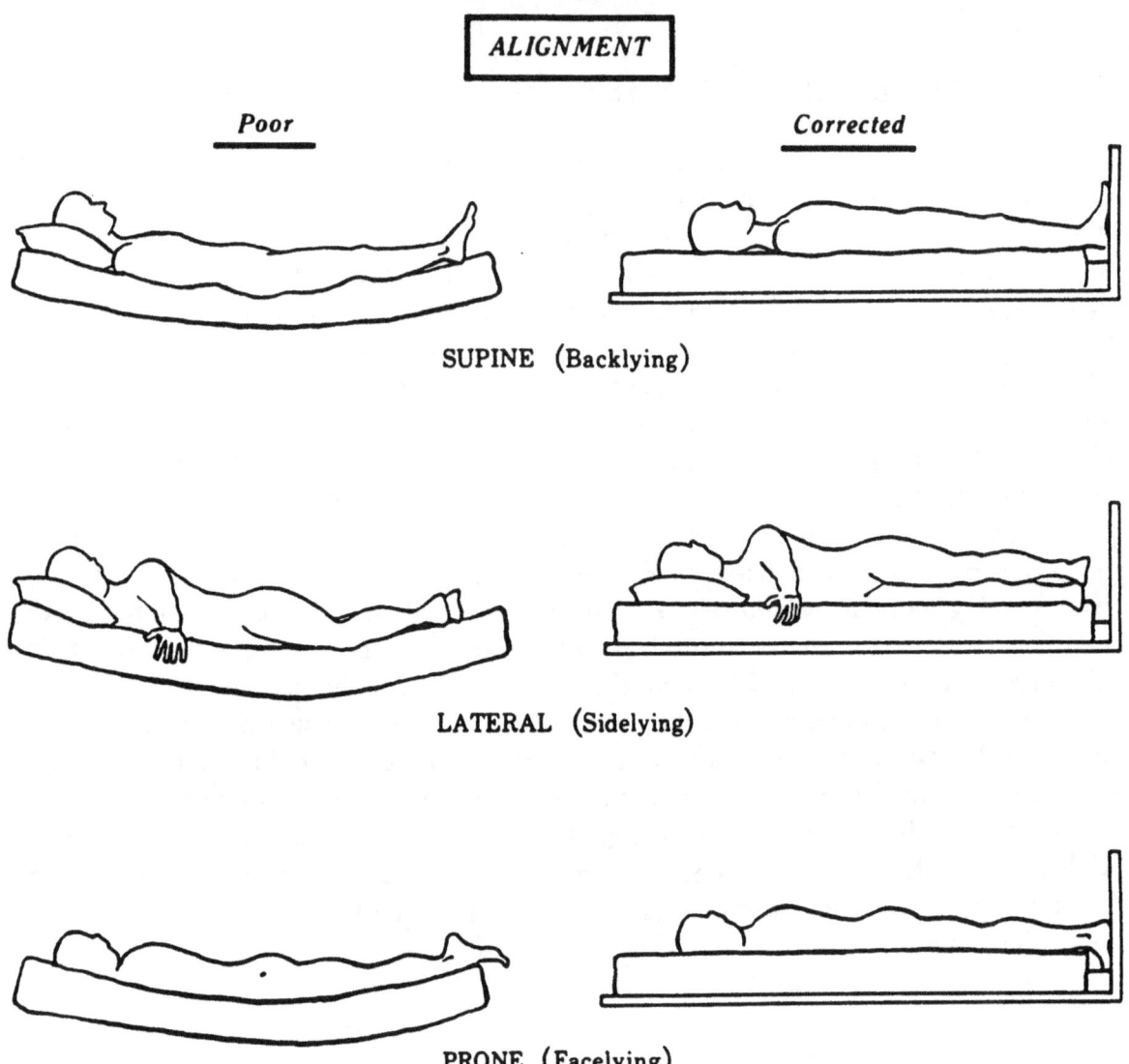

SUPINE (Backlying)

LATERAL (Sidelying)

PRONE (Facelying)

By using small pads, pillows, rolled towels, etc., support may be given to parts of the body, such as shoulders, hips, knees, and ankles, to maintain good body alignment and to contribute to the patient's comfort. Sponge rubber rings and "doughnuts" restrict circulation and create other pressure areas; therefore, their use should be discouraged. Air filled rings may be used if they are inflated *partially only,* allowing for a soft moveable surface rather than a firm surface which could restrict circulation to the area. Sandbags may be placed along the sides of the leg (from hip to knee) to prevent the leg from rotating. A trochanter roll may also be used for preventing outward rotation of the legs. This roll is made by folding either a bath blanket or sheet in quarters lengthwise and placing it crosswise of the bed, centering it under the patient at the hip line. The two ends of the blanket or sheet are then under-rolled firmly against the thigh and tucked slightly under the hip to hold the leg in good alignment.

Pillows supporting upper arm and leg in good alignment

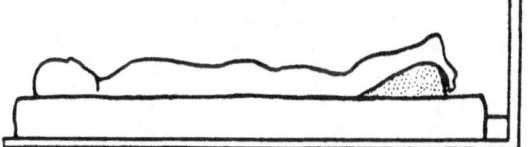

Pillow used to keep good foot alignment and also relax knees by slight flexing

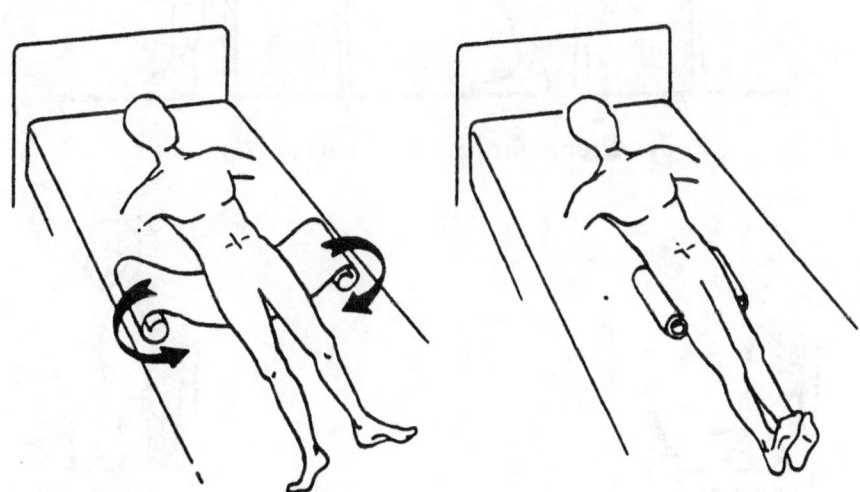

Trochanter Roll

GOOD BODY ALIGNMENT IN A SITTING POSITION

To maintain good body alignment and comfort in a sitting position, the patient's body weight should be equally distributed on his thighs and buttocks. His lower back should be positioned against the back of the chair and his feet flat on the floor. Armrests used to support the arms can help balance the body in a sitting position. If safety belts are necessary to keep the patient in the chair, be certain they are placed in such a manner that good body alignment is maintained. (Pillows and footstools may be used for correcting sitting alignment.)

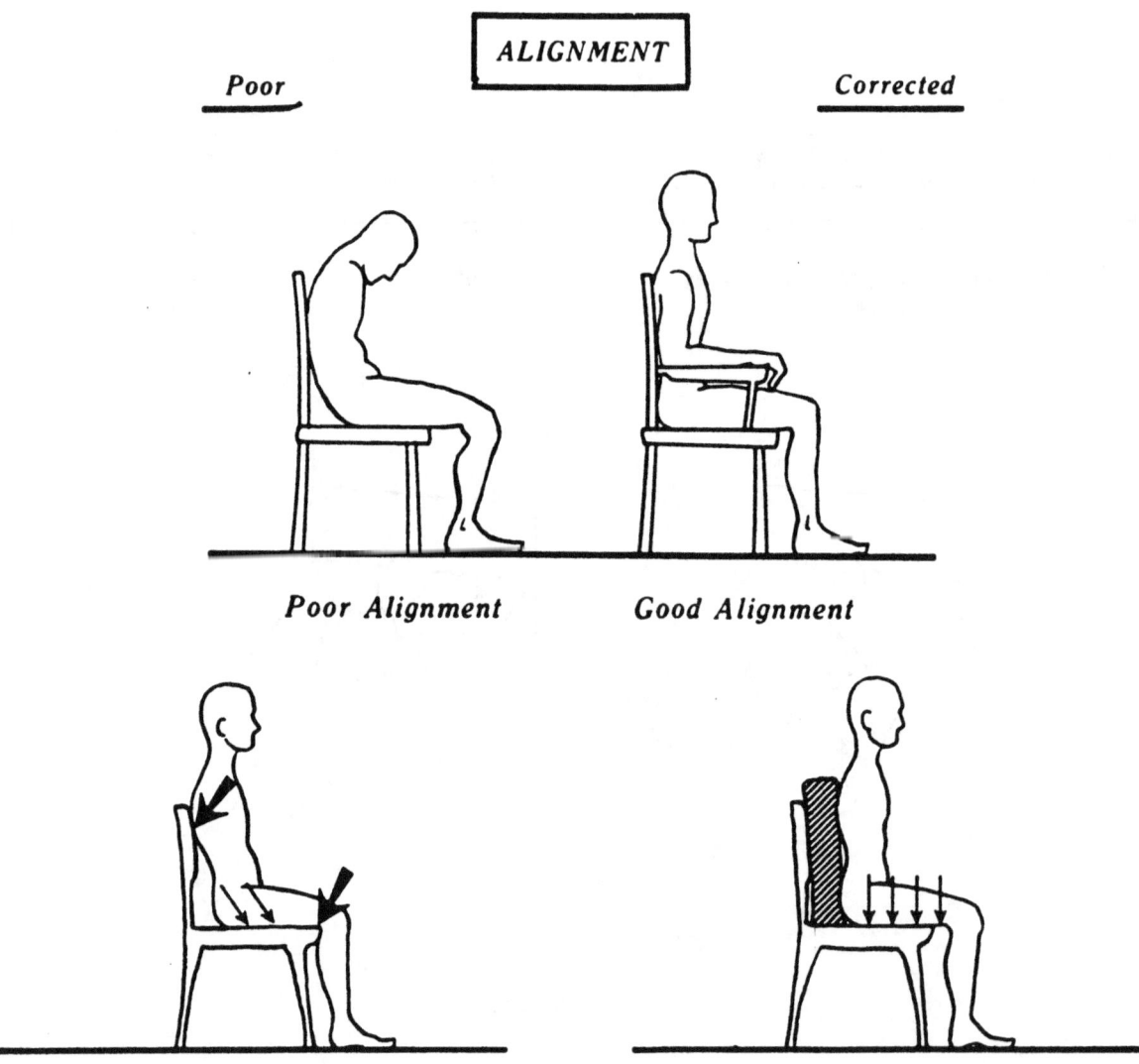

Chair seat too long

Good Body Alignment in a Sitting Position—continued

Poor   *Corrected*

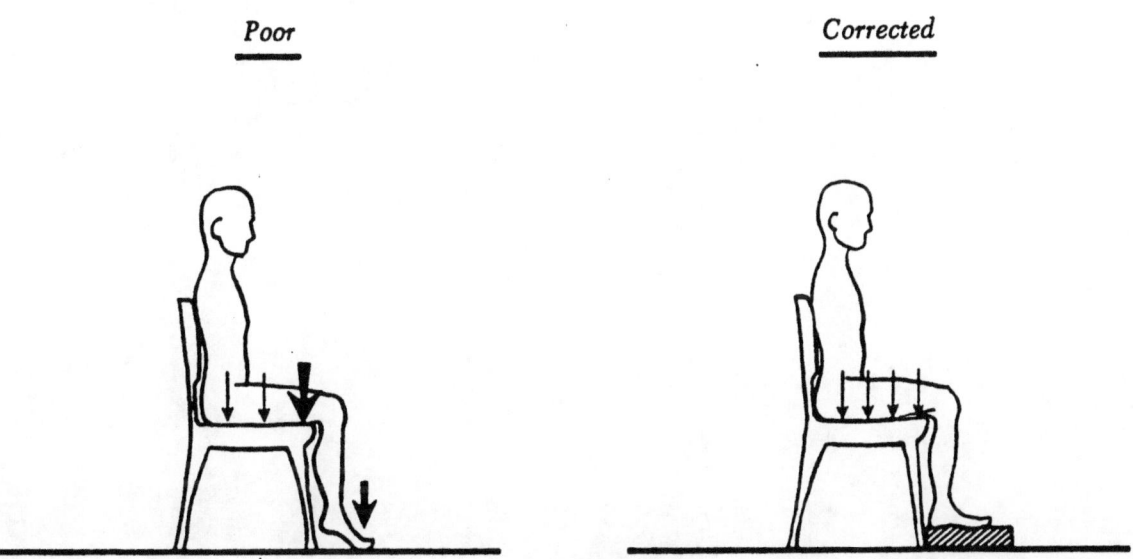

Chair seat too high

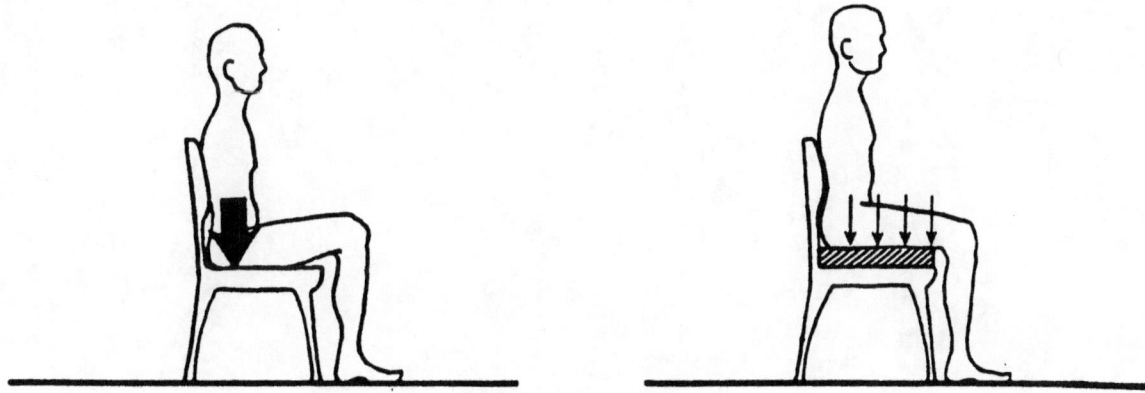

Chair seat too short

Introduction to Exercises

RANGE OF MOTION

Range of motion (R.O.M.) is the extent of movement within a given joint, and motion in a joint is achieved through the action of muscles or groups of muscles. Each joint has a normal range.

A range of motion of particular importance in rehabilitation nursing is the *functional* range. This is the range which is less than normal but which enables the limited joint or combination of joints to be functional for performing activities of daily living.

TYPES OF MOTION EXERCISES

Passive R.O.M. Exercises are done completely by someone other than the patient.

Active Assistive R.O.M. Exercises are done partially by the patient and partially by an assistant or by mechanical equipment.

Free Active R.O.M. Exercises are done wholly by the patient using the muscles of the part of the body being exercised.

Resistive R.O.M. Exercises are active exercises done by the patient against resistance provided by an assistant or by mechanical equipment.

PURPOSES FOR USE OF EXERCISES

(For a better understanding of the stated purpose, examples of types of patients are given; however, use of exercises is not limited to these examples.)

To maintain normal range of motion for all patients. ("Maintain" in this instance means that range of motion exercises are started *early* in the patient's illness or disability.

To increase joint motion to the greatest possible range. For all patients who have limited range of motion, such as arthritic patients who commonly have limitation of elbow or knee joints; for post-fracture patients after periods of immobility of joints.

To maintain muscle strength. Particularly important for the bedridden patient.

To increase muscle strength. Helpful for the patient with any degree of weakness such as loss of muscle strength resulting from long periods of inactivity, and for patient who needs to increase muscle strength to use mechanical devices or artificial limbs.

To increase endurance. Endurance differs from strength in that a patient may have the strength to perform an activity a few times but does not have the endurance to continue performing the activity over a prolonged period of time. Increasing his endurance helps the patient who has developed the strength to stand or walk on crutches but is unable to continue doing so throughout an entire day.

To develop coordination. This is helpful for the patient who has involvement of the nervous system, whether of the spinal cord or of the brain.

To prevent deformities. Limited joint range is one cause of deformities. The importance of starting exercise early before deformities develop cannot be overstressed, especially for hemiplegic, arthritic, and fracture patients.

To promote circulation. This is helpful in diseases of the blood vessels and veins of the extremities such as commonly found in the diabetic patient and the patient with hardening of the arteries (arteriosclerosis). Improved circulation helps to prevent open sores and swelling of extremities. Good circulation promotes bone formation and thus aids in healing fractures. It also improves the functioning of all organs in the body; tones up the muscles of the cardiovascular system; increases oxygen need causing the breathing mechanism to increase its work and eventually its efficiency.

GUIDES IN THE USE OF EXERCISES

In each exercise session include the repetition of every motion of a joint two to five times, repeating the exercise sessions once or twice daily. This is better than irregular or long periods of exercise done less often.

Before starting the exercises explain to the patient —

- What you are doing.
- Why you are doing it.
- What he should do —
    Relax for passive exercises, particularly if stretching is included.
    Help, if active assistive exercise is indicated.
- How it will feel.

During exercise session —

- See that all movements are made in a smooth and steady manner.
- See that all movements are as complete as possible.
- Avoid causing excessive pain.
- Avoid causing excessive fatigue.
- Give patient confidence in your ability.
- Encourage patient to become self-confident.
- Gain the concentration and cooperation of the patient.
- Stop the session if unfavorable change occurs, or if doubtful of patient reaction.

After exercise session —

- Report any change immediately.
- Note change.

Normal Body Motions

The purpose of this section is to acquaint nursing home staff with normal ranges of motion and to provide descriptions of the motions.

NEUTRAL POSITION

This position is used as a basis for describing and performing the body motions. Neutral position is standing or lying straight, heels together, arms at the side with palms toward body.

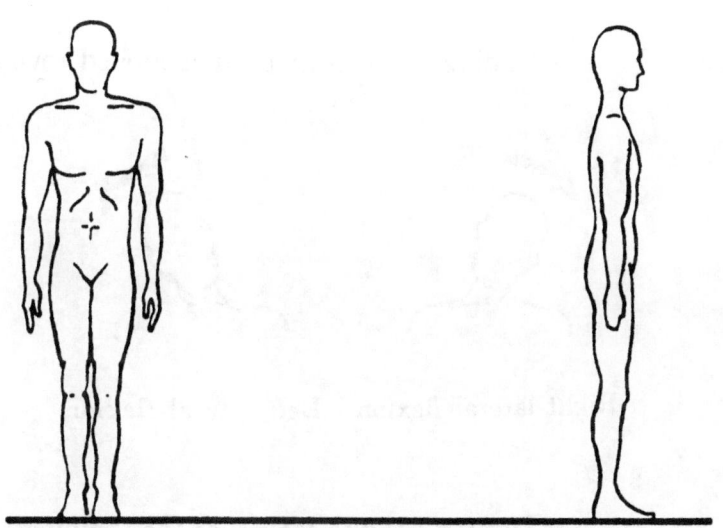

Neutral Position

DEFINITIONS OF COMMON TERMS USED IN DESCRIBING BODY MOTIONS

R.O.M.	— Range of motion: the extent of movement within a given joint.
Flexion	— Bending.
Extension	— Straightening.
Abduction	— Moving the part away from the midline.
Adduction	— Adding to or bringing the part toward the midline.
Rotation	— Turning a limb or body part around its long axis.

MOTIONS OF THE HEAD AND NECK

Extension — Bending head backward (looking up).
Flexion — Bending head forward (looking down).

Extension   Flexion

Lateral Flexion — Bending head so that ear is moved toward shoulder.

Right lateral flexion   Left lateral flexion

Rotation — Turning head to look over the shoulder.

Right rotation   Left rotation

MOTIONS OF THE BODY TRUNK

Flexion — Bending forward from the waist.
Extension — Straightening from the flexed position to the neutral position.
Hyperextension — Moving trunk backward from the waist.

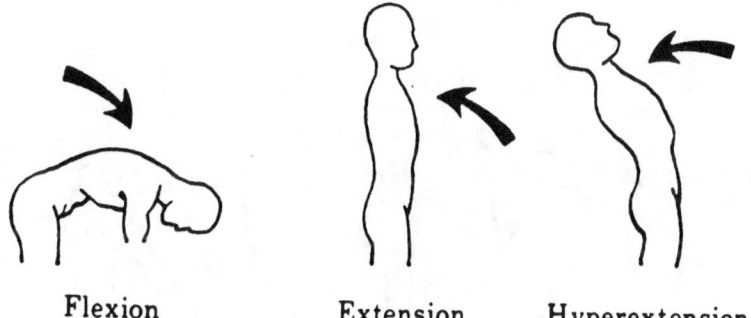

Flexion   Extension   Hyperextension

Lateral Flexion — Bending sideways from the waist.

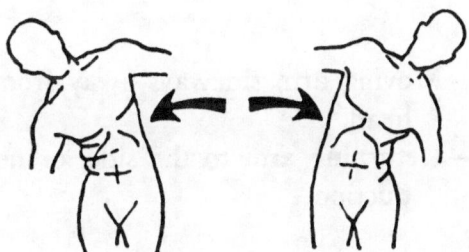

Right lateral flexion   Left lateral flexion

Rotation — Turning shoulders keeping hips stationary, or turning hips keeping shoulders stationary.

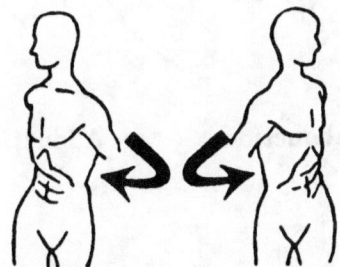

Right rotation   Left rotation

MOTIONS OF THE SHOULDER

Forward Flexion — Moving arm forward and upward until it is along the side of the head.

Extension — Returning arm downward to the side, or neutral position, after flexion.

Hyperextension — Moving arm backward from the neutral position.

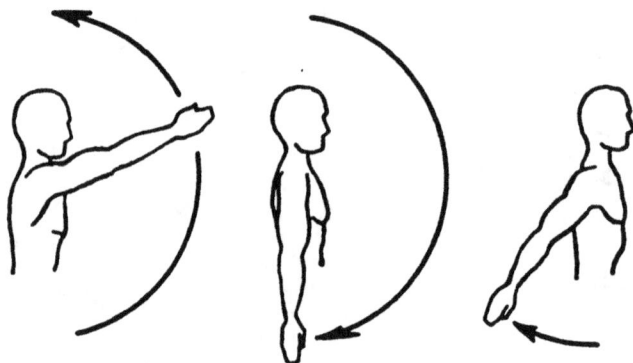

Forward flexion   Extension   Hyperextension

Abduction — Moving arm sideways away from the body to above the head.

Adduction — Returning arm to the side, or neutral position, after abduction.

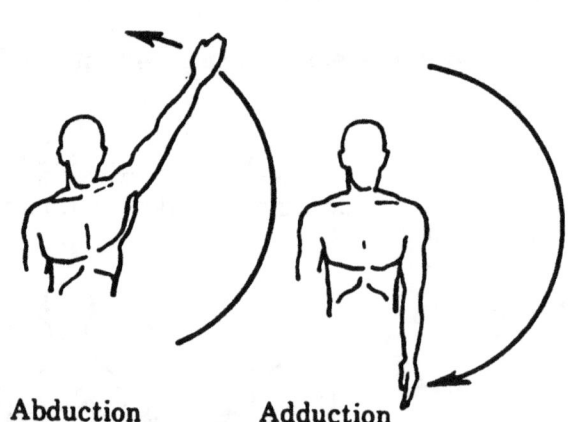

Abduction   Adduction

Motions of the Shoulder—continued

External Rotation — With arm at shoulder height, elbow bent to 90° angle, palm toward feet — turning upper arm until the palm and forearm face forward.

Internal Rotation — With arm at shoulder height, elbow bent to 90° angle, palm toward feet — turning upper arm until palm and forearm face backward.

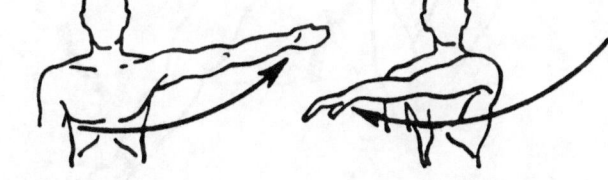

Horizontal Abduction — With arm at shoulder height — moving arm back at this height as far as possible.

Horizontal Adduction — With arm at shoulder height — moving arm across body toward other shoulder as far as possible.

Horizontal abduction   Horizontal adduction

Elevation   — Lifting shoulder toward the ear.
Depression   — Lowering shoulder toward the hip.

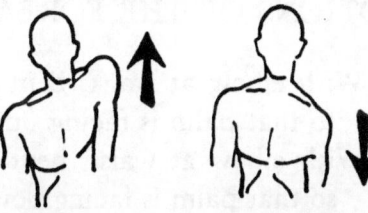

Elevation   Depression

Motions of the Shoulder—*continued*

Protraction — With arm in forward flexion at shoulder height — reaching forward as far as possible.

Retraction — Drawing arm and shoulder back from position of protraction as far as possible.

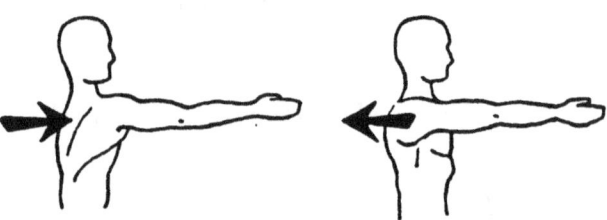

Protraction   Retraction

MOTIONS OF THE ELBOW

Flexion — Bending elbow bringing forearm and hand toward shoulder.

Extension — Returning forearm and hand to neutral position (arm straight).

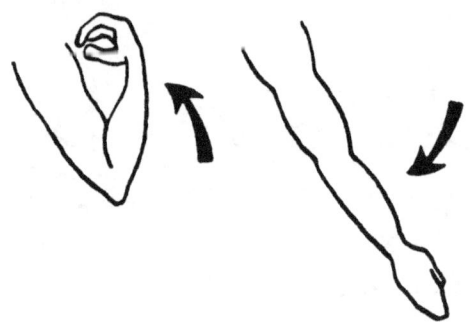

Flexion   Extension

MOTIONS OF THE FOREARM

Supination — With elbow at waist, bent to 90° angle — turning hand so that palm is facing up.

Pronation — With elbow at waist, bent to 90° angle — turning hand so that palm is facing down.

Motions of the Forearm—continued

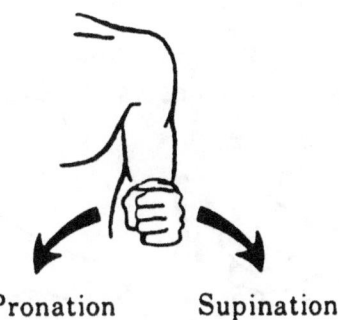

Pronation   Supination

MOTIONS OF THE WRIST

Flexion — Bending wrist so that palm is toward forearm.
Extension — Straightening from flexed position to a neutral position.
Hyperextension — Moving hand so that back of hand is moved toward forearm.

Flexion   Extension   Hyperextension

Radial Deviation — Moving hand sideways so that thumb side of hand is moved toward forearm.
Ulnar Deviation — Moving hand sideways so that little finger side of hand is moved toward the forearm.

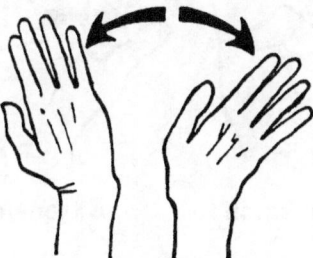

Radial deviation   Ulnar deviation

MOTIONS OF THE FINGERS

Flexion — Bending fingers toward palm (make a fist).
Extension — Returning fingers to neutral position (straighten fingers).

Flexion   Extension

Abduction — Moving fingers apart (spread fingers).
Adduction — Moving fingers together.

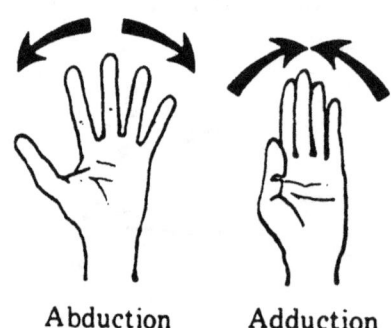

Abduction   Adduction

MOTIONS OF THE THUMB

Flexion — Bending thumb at all joints.
Extension — Straightening thumb.

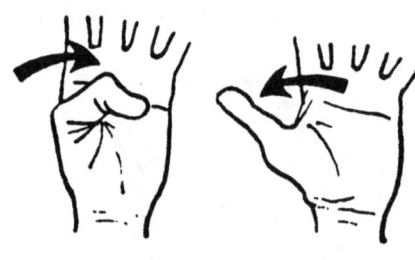

Flexion   Extension

Motions of the Thumb—*continued*

    Abduction   — Palm up, moving thumb up and away from palm.
    Adduction   — Returning thumb to position along side of first finger.

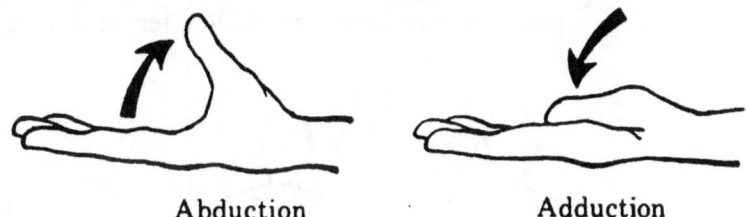

Abduction   Adduction

    Opposition   — Moving thumb out and around to touch little finger.

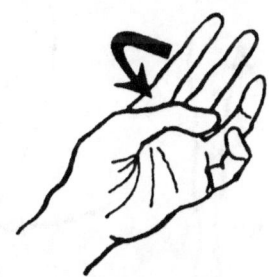

Opposition

MOTIONS OF THE HIP

    Flexion   — Bending hip by moving the leg forward as far as possible.
    Extension   — Returning leg from the flexed hip position to the neutral position.
    Hyperextension   — Moving leg backward from the body as far as possible.

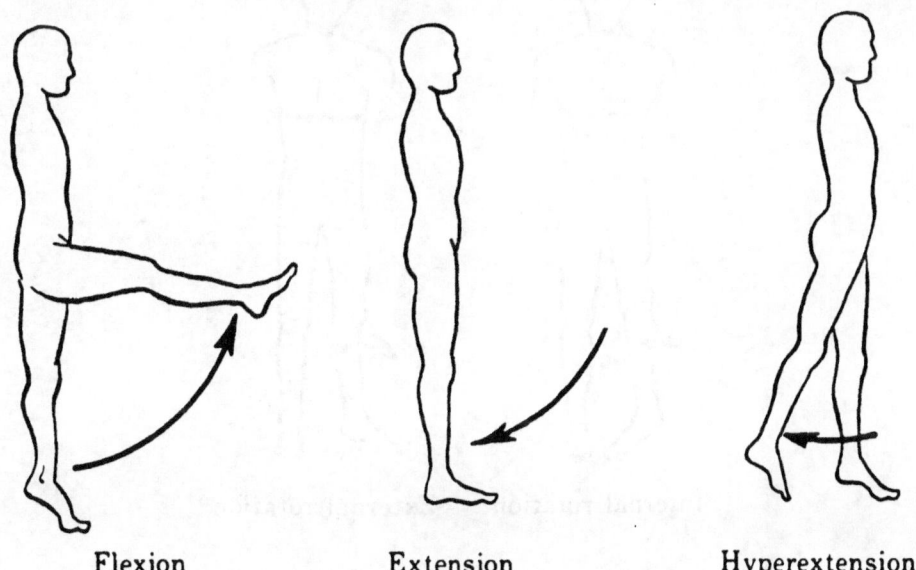

Flexion   Extension   Hyperextension

Motions of the Hip—continued

    Abduction   — Moving leg outward from the body as far as possible.
    Adduction   — Returning leg from the abducted position to the neutral position and across the other leg as far as possible.

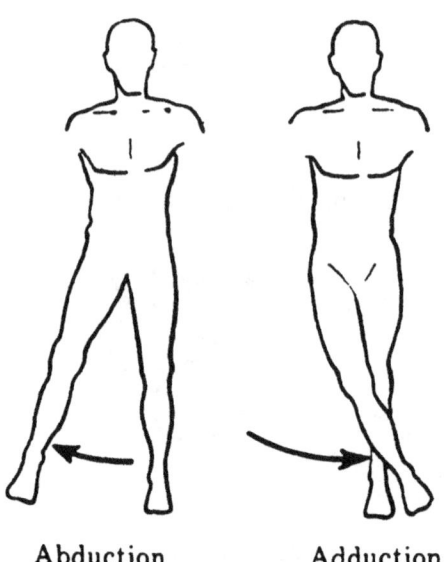

    Abduction   Adduction

    Internal Rotation   — Turning leg in an inward motion so toes point in.
    External Rotation   — Turning leg in an outward motion so toes point out.

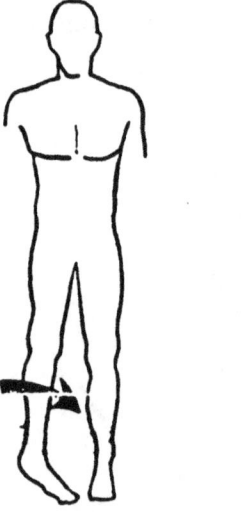 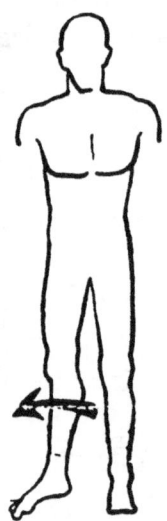

    Internal rotation   External rotation

MOTIONS OF THE KNEE

Flexion — Bending knee bringing lower leg and foot toward back of upper leg.

Extension — Returning lower leg and foot to neutral position (leg straight).

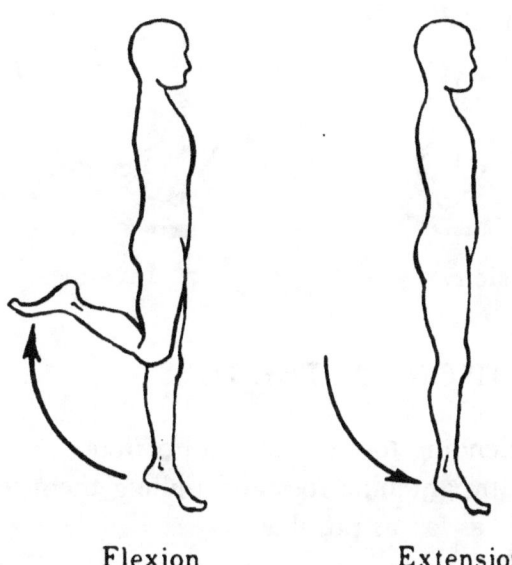

Flexion   Extension

MOTIONS OF THE ANKLE

Dorsal Flexion — Moving foot up and toward the leg.
Plantar Flexion — Moving foot down and away from the leg.

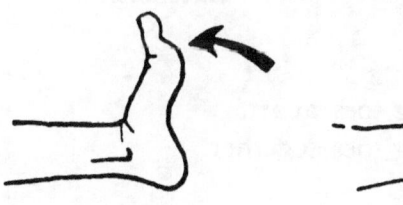

Dorsal flexion   Plantar flexion

Motions of the Ankle—continued

Eversion — Moving foot so sole is facing outward.
Inversion — Moving foot so sole is facing inward.

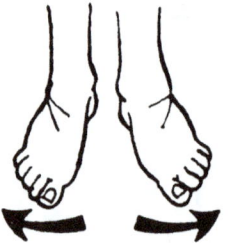 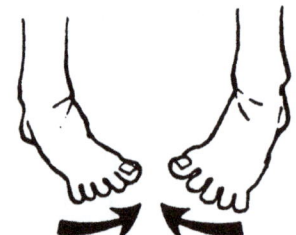

Eversion   Inversion

MOTIONS OF THE TOES

Flexion — Bending toes toward ball of foot.
Extension — Straightening toes and pulling them toward the shinbone as far as possible.

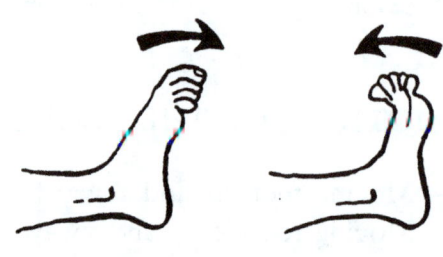

Flexion   Extension

Abduction — Moving toes apart.
Adduction — Moving toes together.

Abduction   Adduction

Passive Range of Motion Exercises

The purpose of this section is to acquaint the nursing home staff with passive range of motion exercises.

POSITIONS OF PATIENT

Supine (backlying) — Lying straight on back with heels together and arms at sides.

Lateral (sidelying) — Lying on side with bottom leg flexed for balance in side position.

Prone (facelying) — Lying on stomach with toes over end of mattress and arms at sides.

GUIDES IN THE USE OF EXERCISES

- Explain to the patient what you are going to do and why.

- Watch patient's face, particularly the eyes, for any expression of pain. Explain that initially the exercises may be painful but the pain will usually subside when exercises are done daily.

- Support the part being exercised above and below the joint for ease in handling and to prevent undue discomfort for the patient.

- Avoid unnecessary stress and strain on yourself by practicing proper body mechanics. Examples: Moving patient to a place on the bed where he can be reached easily; keeping your back as straight as possible; bending your knees as necessary to prevents strain on your back.

- Keep the part of the patient's body you are exercising as close to your body as possible.

- Include in each exercise session the repetition of every motion of the joint two to five times for the joints needing treatment. Exercises should be done a minimum of once a day, and twice a day would be even better.

TECHNIQUES OF PASSIVE RANGE OF MOTION EXERCISES
Supine (backlying) Position

NOTE: The exercises in the following techniques will be designated by motion name only; for description of motion, refer to pages 21 through 32.

Head and neck. Cup hands over patient's ears, grasping head firmly for —

- Flexion
- Lateral Flexion
- Rotation

Trunk. Place one arm under patient's head, grasping far shoulder with one hand and near shoulder with your other hand (or grasp both legs at the knees with one or both arms) for —

- Flexion
- Extension
- Lateral flexion
- Rotation

Shoulder. Grasp patient's arm by placing one hand just above the elbow and your other hand supporting patient's wrist and hand for —

- Forward flexion
- Extension
- Abduction
- Adduction
- Horizontal abduction
- Horizontal adduction
- Elevation
- Depression
- Protraction
- Retraction

With patient's shoulder at 90° abduction and elbow at 90° flexion, use above grasp for —

- External rotation
- Internal rotation

Elbow. Grasp patient's arm by placing one hand just above the elbow and your other hand supporting patient's wrist and hand for —

    Flexion

    Extension

Forearm. With patient's upper arm resting on the bed and elbow bent at 90° angle, with both hands grasp patient's wrist and hand for —

    Pronation

    Supination

Wrist. Grasp patient's forearm just above the wrist with one hand and use the other to grasp the patient's hand for —

    Flexion

    Extension

    Hyperextension

    Radial deviation

    Ulnar deviation

Fingers. Support patient's forearm and wrist with one hand and use the fingers of your other hand for —

    Flexion

    Extension

Use both hands to grasp patient's fingers for —

    Abduction

    Adduction

Thumb. Support patient's hand and fingers with one hand and grasp his thumb with the other hand for —

    Flexion

    Extension

    Abduction

    Adduction

    Opposition

Hip. Support patient's leg by placing his ankle on your upper arm or shoulder, holding his knee in extension with your hand for —

    Flexion (flexion of the hip should also be done with the knee flexed.)

    Extension

Hip—continued

Support patient's leg by placing one hand under his ankle and the other hand just above his knee for —

- Abduction
- Adduction

With patient's leg resting on the bed, place one hand on top of his knee and the other on top of his ankle (or with both the patient's hip and knee flexed at approximately 90° angle, place one hand under his knee and with the other hold his ankle) for —

- Internal rotation
- External rotation

Knee. Flex patient's hip approximately 90° and support his leg by placing one hand just above his knee and grasping his ankle with the other hand for —

- Flexion
- Extension

Ankle. With patient's leg resting on the bed, place one hand on his knee to keep it from flexing and grasp his heel in the palm of your other hand with the sole of his foot resting against your forearm for —

- Dorsal flexion
- Eversion
- Inversion

Toes. Hold patient's foot with one hand and use the other hand for —

- Flexion
- Extension

Use both hands to grasp patient's toes for —

- Abduction
- Adduction

LATERAL (sidelying) POSITION

Head and neck. Cup hands over patient's ears grasping the head firmly for —

- Extension

Shoulder. Grasp patient's arm, placing one hand just above his elbow and the other hand supporting his wrist and hand for —

>Hyperextension
>
>Completion of horizontal abduction
>
>Completion of retraction

Hip. Stand behind patient; stabilize his pelvis with one hand and support his leg on the opposite forearm, grasping his knee with your hand for —

>Hyperextension

Knee. Stand behind patient, keep his hip in extension with one hand and grasp his ankle with your other hand for —

>Flexion (it is necessary that flexion of the knee be done with the hip in extension, lateral or prone position, in addition to the hip in flexion as described under supine position. See "knee," page 36).

Prone (facelying) Position

Trunk. With your hand and arm grasp patient's head and shoulders or both legs for —

>Hyperextension

Shoulder. Place hand under patient's shoulder and lift for —

>Completion of retraction (usually both of patient's shoulders are retracted at the same time when he is in this position.)

All of the remaining range of motion exercises listed for the patient in the lateral position can also be accomplished in a prone position using the same technique.

EDITORIAL NOTE

Although this manual is a guide for training nursing personnel, some sections are directed to the patient in the development of self-care. Directions to the patient will appear in the same typeface as this editorial note.

Transfer Activities

Transfer activities are a valuable aid to the nursing home staff and are beneficial to the patient in the development of patient self-care.

GENERAL PRINCIPLES

BED TO BED

Moving from side to side. Move head and shoulders first by using a "worm-like" movement, then bring hips in line with head and shoulders, using hands if necessary, and follow through with legs by using whatever method is feasible.

Rolling over. Lie on back, arms at sides, knees straight if possible; do not lie too close to edge of bed. Turn body to side by using opposite arm to grasp the mattress or a bedrail and *pull* body to the side position; or continue on to the prone position as desired. To return, use opposite arm to *push* body back to the supine position.

Sitting up with legs still in the bed.

Without mechanical aid —

Lie flat on back, place palms of hands near hips, press on elbows raising head and shoulders, slide elbows back as far as possible under shoulders. Push on hands straightening elbows one at a time, then take small steps forward with hands until you are sitting upright. To lie down reverse the procedure.

With mechanical aid — .

Trapeze—Grasp the bar with one or both hands and pull body to sitting position. Bed rope (made out of three substantial strips of sheeting or unbleached muslin braided together and attached securely to the foot of the bed.)—Grasp the rope with one or both hands placed as far down on the rope as possible and pull body to sitting position.

NOTE: While in the sitting position, begin to practice "push up" exercises to strengthen muscles needed for future transfer activities. Place hands on bed next to hips, straightening elbows, pushing on the bed and raising hips.

Moving from side to side and forward and backward in the sitting position. Place hands on bed next to hips, straighten elbows; push on hands thus raising hips, and slide body from side to side or forward and backward on the bed.

Bed to Bed Transfer—continued

Moving from sitting position with legs extended to dangling position with legs flexed over side of bed. From a balanced sitting position, move legs over the side of the bed using hands as necessary. (This position is used to stimulate circulation of the lower extremities and also to continue improvement of sitting balance.)

CAUTION: You may become dizzy when first assuming this position; do not attempt it unless someone is in attendance.

BED TO WHEELCHAIR

Forward position. Place wheelchair as close to the bed as possible in the forward position facing the bed; *lock brakes.* Move into sitting position with legs extended crosswise of bed away from chair; with hands placed on armrests of chair, push on hands and arms and slide body backwards into wheelchair, lifting legs off bed to chair position. Returning to the bed, reverse the procedure.

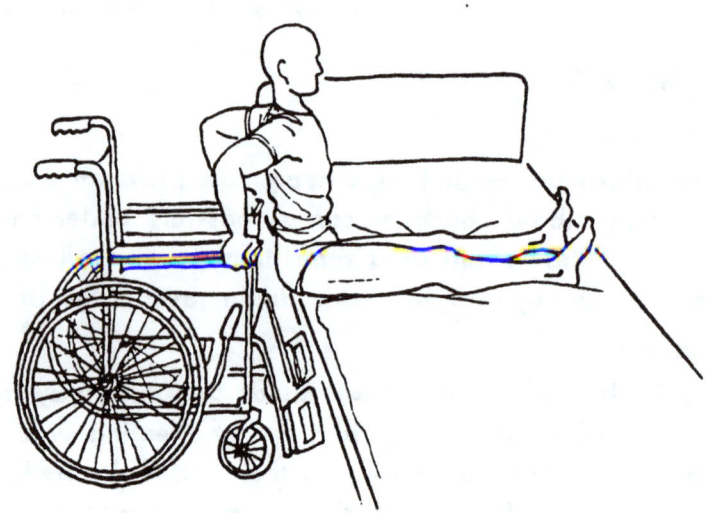

Angle position. Place wheelchair as close to the bed as possible in an angle position facing the bed; *lock brakes.* Move into dangling position with legs in the space between wheelchair and bed; place hand closest to wheelchair on the far armrest of the chair and other hand beside hips on the bed; using a pivot movement, bearing weight of body on hands and arms, lift body into wheelchair. Returning to the bed, reverse the procedure.

NOTE: With the wheelchair in this position, the slide board can be used as a bridge in transferring from bed to wheelchair.

Bed to Wheelchair—continued

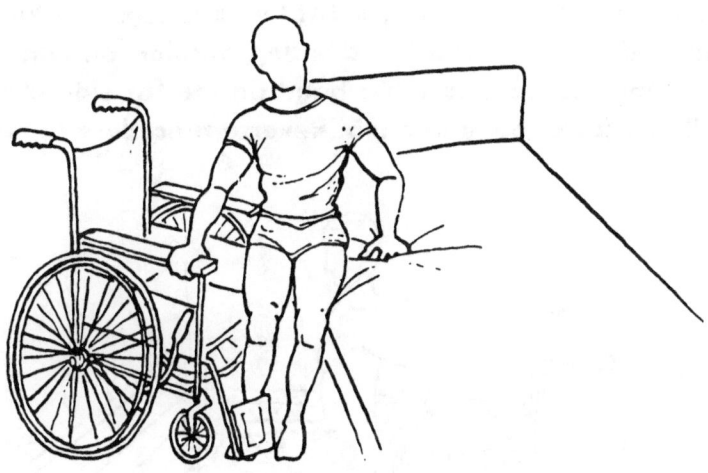

WHEELCHAIR TO CHAIR

Place wheelchair facing the chair, as close to the chair as possible, with footrests of wheelchair straddling one front leg of the chair; *lock brakes.* Slide forward to edge of wheelchair, place one hand on armrest of wheelchair and other hand on seat of chair; using a pivot movement bearing weight of body on hands and arms, lift body into the chair. Reverse procedure for returning to wheelchair.

NOTE: The same procedure can be used in transferring from wheelchair to toilet seat and to shower chair or bench.

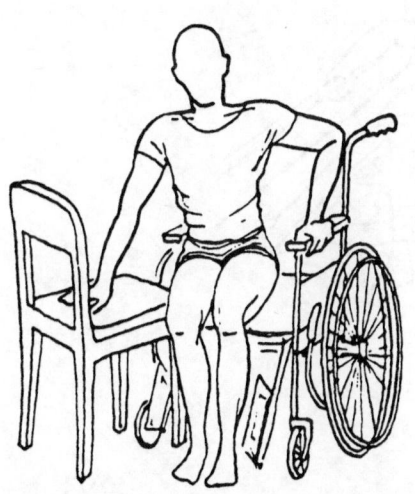 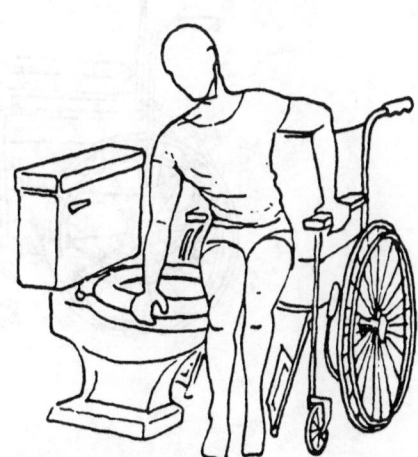

WHEELCHAIR TO BATHTUB

Forward position. Place wheelchair as close as possible to the side or end of bathtub in forward position facing tub; *lock brakes.* Lift feet and legs into tub. Placing hands on armrests of chair, slide body forward to a sitting position on edge of tub. Place one hand on the near edge of tub and other hand on the far side of tub or on grabrail mounted on wall and lower body into tub. Reverse procedure to return to chair.

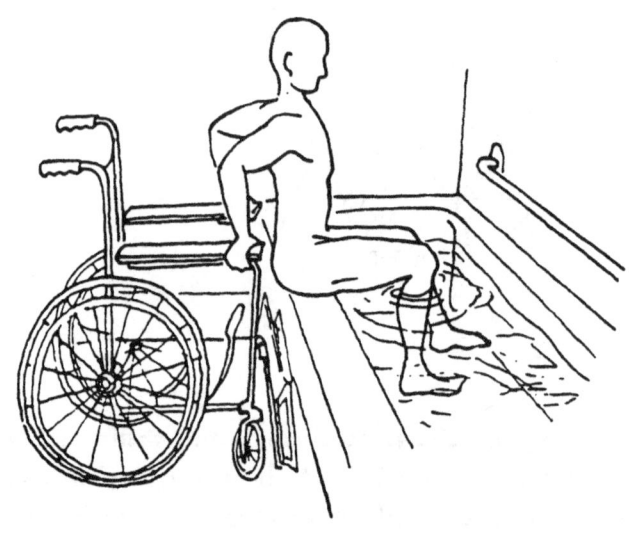

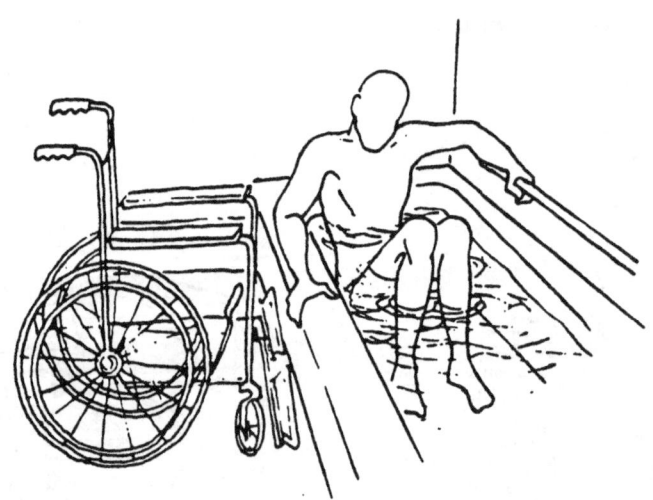

Wheelchair to Bathtub—*continued*

Angle or side position. Place wheelchair as close to bathtub as possible in either an angle position or side position facing the faucet end of the tub; *lock brakes.* Lift feet and legs into tub. Slide sideways from wheelchair to a sitting position on edge of tub. Place one hand on the near edge of tub and other hand on the far edge or on grabrail mounted on the wall and lower body into tub. Reverse procedure to return to chair.

NOTE: With the wheelchair in this position, a slide board or bench can be used as a bridge in transferring from wheelchair to tub.

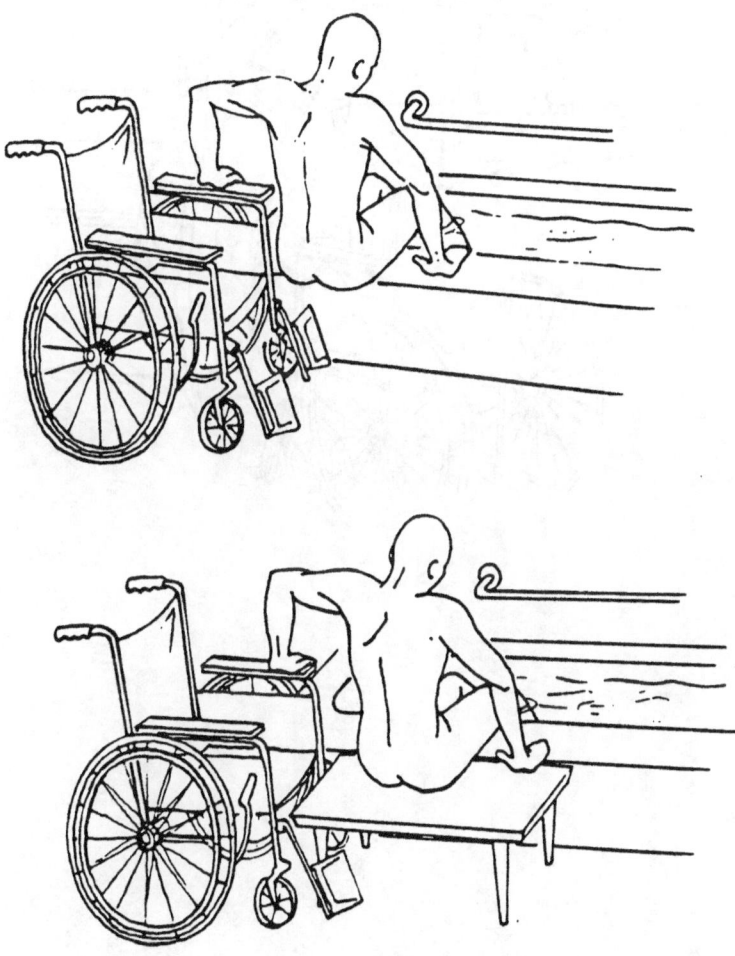

Helpful Hints: If tub is filled with water, it is easier for you to get in and out, but caution must be used. To prevent slipping in the tub, a rubber suction bath mat can be used. Also a small stool equipped with suction crutch tips may be used in the bathtub if it is difficult for you to lower yourself to the bottom of the tub.

WHEELCHAIR TO AUTOMOBILE

Place wheelchair facing door of the car; open car door and swing it back to lock position. Move wheelchair forward as close as possible into the angle formed by car door and side of the car; *lock brakes.* Slide to front edge of wheelchair seat and, by turning in the direction of the front of the car, face toward wheelchair. Placing hand nearest car door on the window ledge of the door and other hand on wheelchair armrest farthest from the door, lift yourself onto the car seat; then lift legs and feet into the car. Reverse procedure for returning to wheelchair.

Ambulation Activities

Ambulation is a difficult task for the patient who has not walked for a long time due to an illness or a disability. The nurse must have a physician's order for ambulation of the patient. She will need to know how to help the patient prepare for ambulation activities and how to teach him to use the necessary equipment. The nurse will gain the patient's interest and cooperation by including him in the planning. Both the patient and the nurse must remember that learning to walk takes time and patience. Learning to use crutches, cane, or walker requires a planned program of progressive activities.

EXERCISES

This series of exercises is given to improve the patient's strength, endurance, and balance.

BED AND CHAIR
- Raise head and shoulders off the bed, reaching forward with hands.
- Sit up in bed, place hands on bed next to hips and do "push up" exercises Books or blocks may be used under the hands to improve the mechanics of the exercise.

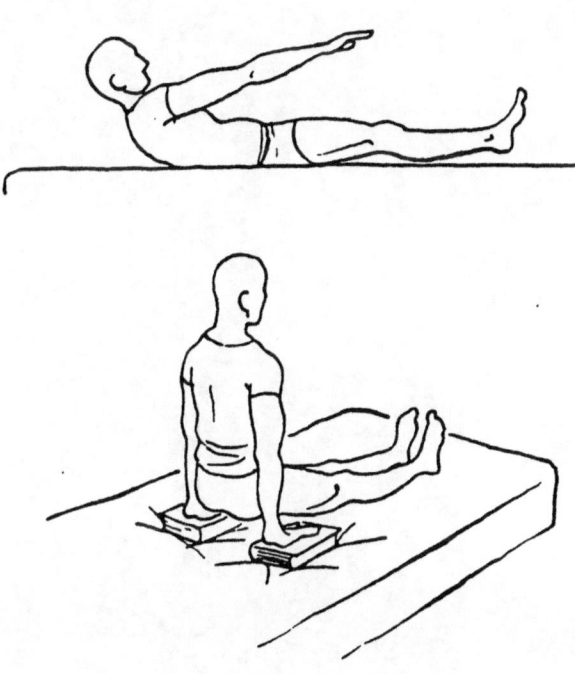

Bed and Chair—continued

- Grasp arms of chair with hands and raise body out of seat.

NOTE: Chair may be a wheelchair (locked brakes) or any type of armchair. Propelling your own wheelchair helps to strengthen your arms.

 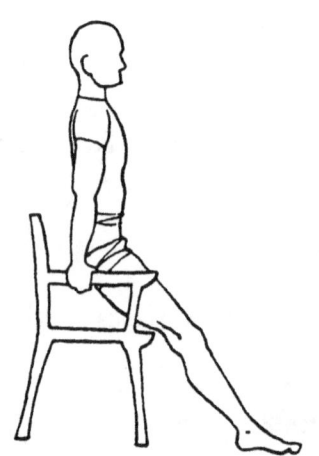

PARALLEL BARS

- Propel the wheelchair into the parallel bars; *lock brakes.* Use the bars to push up to the standing position, do not *pull* up to stand.

- Standing balance —
  With hands grasping bars, shift body weight from side to side.
  Shifting body weight from side to side, alternately lift one hand then the other.
  Remove both hands from bars and stand alone as long as possible.

- Push-ups—grip bars with hands and raise body.

- Shift body weight forward and backward placing hands on the bars in front of body and then on the bars in back of body.

- Turn between the bars by pivoting the body part way to face one bar; grasp that bar with both hands, then turn part way again. Place one hand on each bar and complete body turn.

NOTE: If parallel bars are not available, two heavy chairs, the ends of beds, stationary furniture, hall rail and chair, or other substitutes can be used. Be certain that any substitute used is stable and can't be easily overturned. Do same exercises as described above.

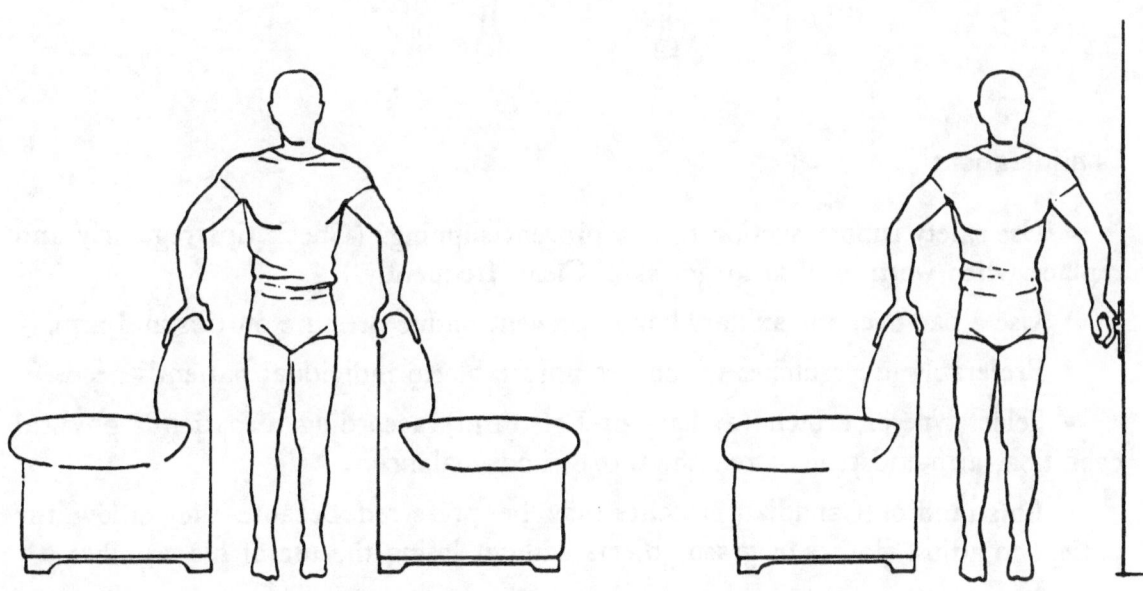

GAIT

CRUTCHES

Types

Axillary — fits under the upper arm.

Lofstrand or Canadian — fits the forearm by means of a metal cuff.

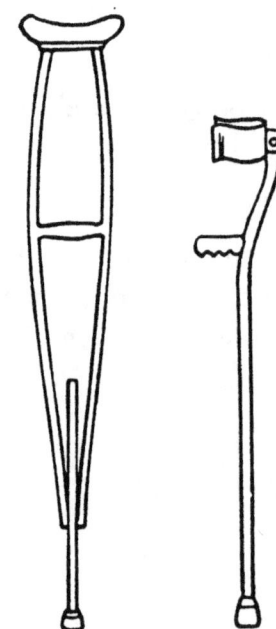

Considerations

• Use safety rubber suction tips to prevent slipping. (Check tips regularly and replace when worn and no longer safe. Clean frequently.)

• Use a pad over the axillary bar to prevent undue pressure on ribs and arm.

• Preferably use crutches which are adjustable to individual patient's needs.

• Select type of crutch (axillary or Lofstrand) according to patient's physical condition, arm and trunk strength, and/or body balance.

• Lofstrand or Canadian crutches may be preferred because they allow the patient to adjust clothes or grasp objects without losing the use of his crutches.

• Do not allow patient to use crutches alone unless he has demonstrated the ability to use them correctly and safely.

Measurements (Do not give patient crutches until he is properly fitted.)

- *Axillary Crutch.* Measure the length from the armpit to a point 6 inches out from the side of the foot or measure the length from the armpit to foot and add 2 inches.

- Adjust the handbars so the patient's elbows are bent at approximately 30° angle.

NOTE: Either of the above measuring methods may be used with patient lying in bed, standing against the wall, or standing between parallel bars.

- *Lofstrand Crutch.* Adjust the length of the crutch to allow the elbows to be bent at approximately 30° angle with the crutch tips 6 to 8 inches to the side and in front of the foot.

Posture and Position

- Stand as straight as possible.
- Look straight ahead, *not* down at feet.
- Bear body weight on hands, never on armpits, to prevent possible paralysis of hand and arm.
- Hug axillary bar close to body, against rib cage. This is the pivot point for the motion of the crutch.
- Place crutches about 6 to 8 inches in front of and 6 to 8 inches on each side of feet.
- One should be able to place two fingers horizontally between armpit and top of crutch.
- To allow for the proper tripod base never have the crutches and feet in the same line.

Gait Patterns

- *Four Point.* Move right crutch, left foot; left crutch, right foot. It is a simple, slow, but safe method; there are always three points of support on the floor.

- *Two Point.* Move right crutch and left foot simultaneously, then left crutch and right foot simultaneously. This requires more balance than the above method because only two points are supporting the body at any one time.

- *Three Point.* Move both crutches and the weaker lower extremity forward simultaneously and then move the stronger lower extremity forward. It is used by those having one lower extremity which cannot take full or any weight bearing and one extremity which can support the whole body weight.

Gait Patterns—*continued*

- *Tripod Alternate.* Move right crutch, left crutch; drag feet forward (used by those unable to lift either extremity).

- *Tripod Simultaneous* (rocking horse gait). Move both crutches forward simultaneously; drag feet forward (used by those unable to lift either extremity).

- *Swinging To.* Move both crutches forward, then lift and swing body forward just short of the crutches.

- *Swinging Through.* Move both crutches forward, then lift and swing body beyond crutches. Skill, strength, and proper timing are required. Use swinging gait to lift body off the floor when there is a severe disability of the lower extremities.

- *Sideward Four Point.* Move right crutch to the right; right foot to right; left foot to right; left crutch to right.

- *Backward Four Point.* Move left foot back; right crutch back; right foot back; left crutch back.

- *Turning on Crutches.* Place one crutch in front of body, the other slightly to the side and rear; pivot feet or lift body in direction crutches were moved; repeat as often as necessary to make turn.

WALKER

- *Advantage of a walker.* It helps patient who feels the need for the security of the walker.

- *Disadvantages of a walker.* Patient puts so much weight and dependency on the walker while taking steps that it becomes difficult to wean him away from its use. It cannot be used on stairs.

Types

- *Standard* — a rigid four-legged frame used as a mechanical aid for stability and convenience in walking.

- *Reciprocal* — similar to standard in construction with additional feature of a hinge mechanism enabling the patient to move each side forward independently, thus allowing for reciprocal action.

NOTE: It is not advisable to use walkers with wheels as the wheels reduce the stability factor of the walker thus creating a potentially unsafe piece of equipment.

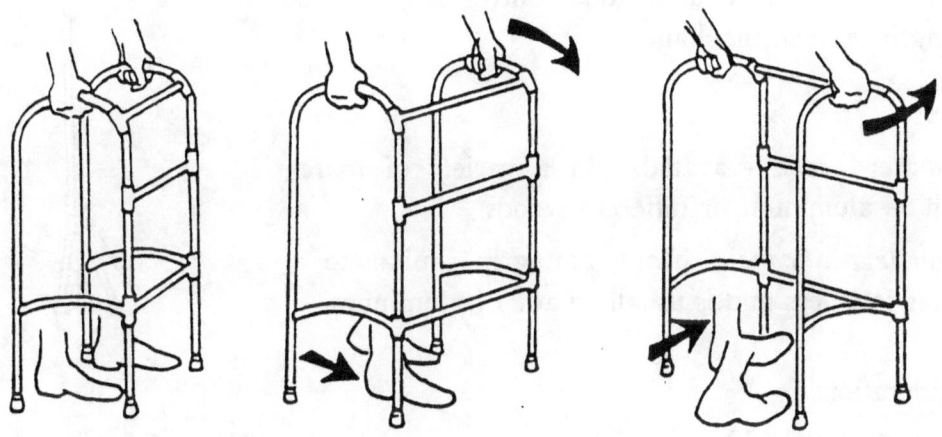

Considerations

- Use safety rubber suction tips to prevent slipping. Check tips regularly and replace when worn and no longer safe. Clean frequently.

- Preferably use walkers which are adjustable to individual patient's needs.

- Do not allow patient to use walker alone unless he has demonstrated the ability to use it correctly and safely.

Measurements

- Adjust the height of the walker to allow elbows to be bent at approximately 30° angle.

Posture and Position
- Stand as straight as possible.
- Look straight ahead, *not* down at feet.

Gait Patterns
- *Standard.* Move walker forward, then right foot, then left foot.
- *Reciprocal.* Use either of the following:
Move right side of walker; then left foot; left side of walker, then right foot; or move right side of walker and left foot simultaneously; then left side of walker and right foot simultaneously.

NOTE: Some crutch patterns may be applied to the walker depending on individual patient needs.

CANE

The use of a cane requires good control of the trunk and strength in arm and hand.

Types

- *Standard cane* — available in a variety of materials such as aluminum or different woods.
- *Four-legged cane* — has a handgrip similar to a shovel, has four legs and is usually made of aluminum.

Considerations

- Use safety rubber suction tips to prevent slipping. Check tips regularly and replace when worn and no longer safe. Clean frequently.
- Preferably use cane which is adjustable to individual patient's needs.
- Select type of cane according to patient's physical condition, arm and trunk strength, and body balance.
- Do not allow patient to use cane alone unless he has demonstrated the ability to use it correctly and safely.

Measurements

- Measure cane according to type of gait pattern used by patient. (See Gait Patterns, page 53).

Posture and Position
- Stand as straight as possible.
- Look straight ahead, not down at feet.

Gait Patterns

• *Mainly for weight bearing.* Carry cane on side of leg; keep elbow stiff and the cane along side of weak leg, bearing part of body weight on the cane as you step forward with good leg. This cane is measured so that the arm can be straight when bearing weight on the cane.

• *Mainly for balance.* Carry the cane on the side opposite to weak leg; move cane forward; weak leg steps forward; good leg forward. This cane is measured to allow for a 30° bend of the elbow.

ELEVATION ACTIVITIES

These procedures are given to enable patient to go from a sitting position to a standing position; to climb stairs, curbs, and ramps.

CHAIRS

Armrests (includes wheelchair and any chair with armrests.)

• *Patient has some leg power.* Place chair, or wheelchair with brakes locked, with back against the wall or a stable surface; slide body to front edge of chair; place better leg back under the edge of the chair. Holding both crutches by the handpieces with one hand and placing the other hand on the armrest of the chair push on hands, straightening the better leg, and bring body to standing position. Balancing on better leg and crutches transfer one crutch and then the other to underarm position. Reverse procedure to return to sitting position.

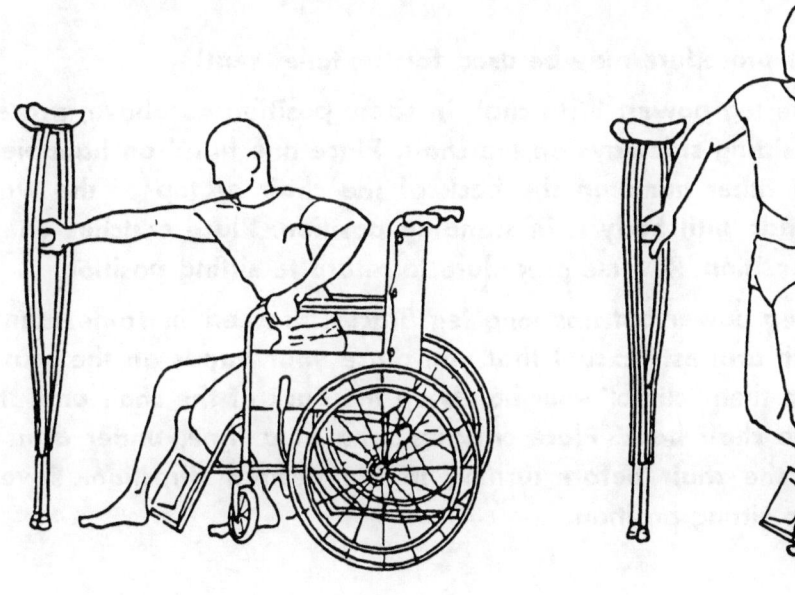

Armrests—*continued*

• *Patient has no leg power but has long leg braces.* Place chair in same position as above; lock one brace at the knee and cross this leg over foot of other leg; turn upper part of the body toward the unlocked leg until the head and shoulders are facing the back of the chair. Grasping the armrests with both hands, push body upwards (this allows the legs to turn in the same direction as the head and shoulders) until leg with locked brace is supporting the body. Lock the brace at knee of other leg. Place crutches under arms, one at a time, shifting body weight from chair to crutches and bring trunk upright. Back up a few steps until crutches are clear of the chair before attempting to turn in the desired direction. Reverse procedure to return to sitting position.

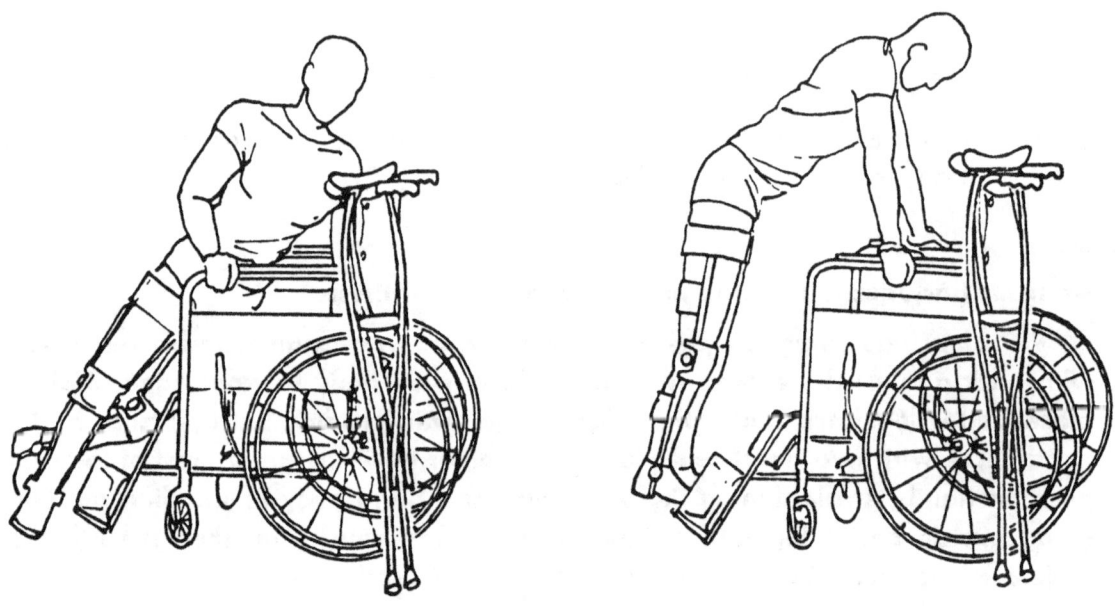

No Armrests (same procedure may be used for the toilet seat)

• *Patient has some leg power.* With chair in same position as above, proceed in same manner but sitting sideways on the chair. Place one hand on handpieces of both crutches and other hand on the back of the chair or top of the water tank, push up on hands until body is in standing position. Place crutches one at a time in underarm position. Reverse procedure to return to sitting position.

• *Patient has no leg power but has long leg braces.* Proceed in same manner as with the chair with armrests except that you place your hands on the seat of the chair initially, and then "climb" your hands up the back of the chair until they are on the top of the chair back. Place crutches, one at a time, under arms as before. Again clear the chair before turning in the desired direction. Reverse procedure to return to sitting position.

STAIRS

- *Patient has some leg power.* Place one hand on bannister and both crutches under opposite arm; balance weight on hands and arms; step up with stronger leg; straighten stronger leg, thus lifting other leg and crutches. Continue up the stairs repeating the same pattern. Going down the stairs, move the crutches forward first then the weaker leg, thus allowing the stronger leg to take the load of lowering the body weight.

- *Patient has no leg power but has long leg braces.* Place one hand on bannister and both crutches under opposite arm. Push on both hands and lift body and legs up the step. Bring crutches up to the step. Repeat in the same pattern up the stairs. Going down the stairs, move the crutches down onto the next step and then, bearing the body weight on the hands, swing both legs down to that step. Proceed in same pattern down the stairs.

CURBS

- *Patient has some leg power.* Approach the curb, secure good balance on the crutches; step up on curb with stronger leg, straighten stronger leg thus lifting the crutches and weaker leg up on the curb. Going down off the curb move the crutches down first, then the weaker leg followed by the stronger leg.

- *Patient has no leg power but has long leg braces.* Back up to the curb and, balancing on the crutches, swing one leg back and upwards onto the curb. Continuing to lean into both crutches, shift weight onto leg which is up on the curb and swing other leg back and upwards onto curb. Bring shoulders back so that body is arched backwards; walk crutches back to edge of curb. Balancing and supporting body on both legs and one crutch, lift the opposite crutch up onto curb; shift weight onto this crutch and bring the second crutch up on the curb. Going down off the curb reverse the procedure.

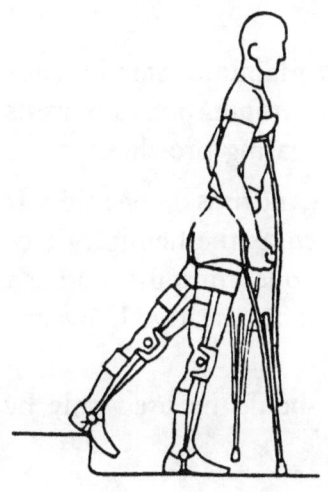 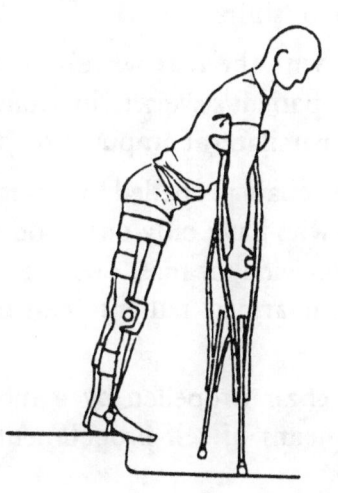 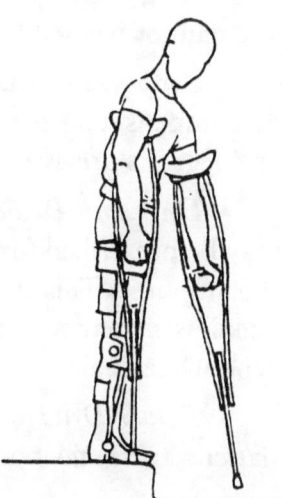

RAMPS

Ascending and descending ramps are not common daily activities; however, since you may have a slanting surface in your home or may encounter sloping sidewalks, it is important that you learn to manipulate your crutches on a ramp.

Ascending and descending may be done by either of two methods —

- Standing facing the ramp, place both crutches separately or simultaneously on ramp. Move body forward by pushing on crutches and advancing feet to position just short of same line as crutches.

- Standing sideways with right shoulder toward the ramp, use the sideways Four Point Gait. Move right crutch to right, right foot to right, left foot to right and left crutch to right. Continue in same pattern up or down the ramp.

WHEELCHAIRS

The wheelchair is used by persons with a variety of handicapping conditions, and a variety of factors must be considered in selecting the proper chair for the individual. The techniques of how to use the wheelchair also vary according to individual patient needs.

CONSIDERATIONS FOR SELECTION

Types

- *Universal* — the chair with the larger wheels in the back. It is used both indoors and outdoors; promotes better posture, permits easier transfer activities, and can be tilted to go up curbs and stairs.

- *Traveler* — the chair with the larger wheels in front. It is used only indoors or on level surfaces; promotes poorer posture; is more difficult for transferring activities and cannot be used for curbs or stairs.

- *Amputee* — the chair with the rear wheels set back. It maintains safe balance by compensating for loss of patient's weight in front due to amputation. Footrests and legrests are available for unilateral amputee or patient wearing prosthesis.

- *One-Arm Drive* — the chair propelled by having both handrims on one side. It may be prescribed for those who have only one good arm, such as the hemiplegic or the amputee. This chair is too wide for most doors, is difficult to learn to use, and is a needless expense as most one-armed patients can be taught to use the Universal type wheelchair.

- *Power-Driven* — the chair propelled by a motor. It should be used only by patients with no possible means of self-propellment.

SIZES

- Adult
- Adult, extra wide
- Junior
- Child

ACCESSORIES

The individual needs of the patient must be the first consideration in selecting the accessories on a wheelchair. These accessories are important factors in accomplishing daily living activities and in maintaining proper body alignment or patient comfort while patient is in the wheelchair. Accessories should be selected by someone able to analyze the patient's disabilities and potential ability.

- *Brakes* — *not* standard equipment on the wheelchair, therefore must be specifically ordered. *Every* wheelchair should be equipped with brakes for the safety of the patient.

- *Wheels* — 5-inch front casters are standard equipment on wheelchairs; however, the 8-inch caster can be ordered and allows for better control of the wheelchair by the patient for turning, rolling over rough surfaces, and maneuvering in small spaces. Handrims with projections can be ordered for the patient who is unable to grasp a regular handrim for propelling his wheelchair.

- *Armrests* — upholstered armrests may be desired for the patient's comfort. Removable arms may be necessary to allow the patient to perform transfer activities. The armrests may be equipped with button locks to increase stability. Desk arms can be ordered if accessibility to a desk or table is necessary.

- *Backrests* — backrests adjustable to partial or full reclining positions may be ordered for the patient who is unable to sit in an upright position all the time. Zipper backs may be ordered for the patient who finds it necessary to slide in and out of the back of the chair for transfer activities. Removable headrest extensions can be ordered for additional back and head support.

- *Legrests* — adjustable legrests may be ordered for the patient who must have one or both extremities elevated. Swinging detachable legrests may be ordered to allow the patient a closer approach in transferring.

- *Footrests* — heel loops which prevent the feet from slipping off the footrest may be ordered for one or both feet as needed. A heel strap may be substituted for individual heel loops if it is necessary for both feet to be held on the footrest. Toe loops for maintaining proper positioning of the foot on the footrest may be ordered.

- *Seat Cushions* — foam rubber seat cushions in 2-inch or 4-inch heights may be ordered for the patient's comfort and as an aid to prevention of pressure areas.

CARE

Proper care of the wheelchair is as important as the care of an automobile. With a little regular attention, the wheelchair can be kept in good condition and its life and usefulness can be prolonged.

- *Cleaning*. Wipe all metal-chrome parts once a week with a damp cloth and protect them with a light coating of a general purpose household oil applied with a soft cloth. Sponge leather upholstery with a damp cloth and clean with saddle soap. Be sure to dry both chrome and leather whenever they are wet.

- *Lubrication*. Oil the center bolt of the cross bars and the attachment of brakes to lower side bars. Grease both front and rear wheel axles with vaseline or any grease lubricant. (This is generally necessary only on a yearly basis.) Apply paraffin wax when needed to any telescoping parts, such as adjustable backs, removable arms, footrests, and extensions. DO NOT OIL OR GREASE THESE PARTS.

- *Miscellaneous*. Be sure to keep nuts, bolts, screws, etc., tight, and if any part breaks have it repaired by an authorized wheelchair repairman. Be sure to use a wheelchair wrench for adjusting footrests.

TECHNIQUES

Using both arms

- *Forward*. Grasp the handrims as far toward the back of the wheels as possible and push both wheels forward at the same time. It is less fatiguing to use long, even strokes to propel wheelchair.

- *Turning*. To turn a corner, push the wheel on the opposite side from the direction you want to turn and hold the other wheel still. To turn around in a small space, place one hand forward on one handrim and the other hand back on the opposite handrim; pull with the forward hand and push with the back hand at the same time.

Using one arm and one leg

- *Forward*. Pushing one wheel only will automatically turn the chair in a circle; therefore, push the wheel with the one good hand and at the same time use the one good foot to pull the chair in opposition, thus countering the turn and allowing the chair to go forward.

- *Turning*. Toward affected side—use only the hand to turn the wheelchair. Toward unaffected side—reach across to the opposite wheel with good hand and, using the foot in the same manner as in the forward movement, turn the wheelchair.

Activities of Daily Living

Activities of daily living are commonly referred to as ADL. They are daily necessities of self-care which are done automatically by the adult, are taught to the child, but which may be neglected by the elderly. The nurse is responsible for determining the reasons why the patient is not performing his self-care activities. The patient may need to be reminded, remotivated, or retrained. Awareness of the specific problem of the individual patient is essential for a successful ADL program.

BASIC SELF-CARE ACTIVITIES (ADL)

BED ACTIVITIES

Moving from side to side when flat in bed.
Rolling from side to side.
Turning over on to abdomen.
Rising from reclining to sitting position.
Turning from sitting position to dangling position.
Obtaining objects from bedside table.
Using trapeze, side rails, bed ropes, clothing, straps.

PERSONAL HYGIENE (GROOMING)

Caring for fingernails.
Washing hands and face.
Caring for teeth (dentures).
Shaving.
Applying cosmetics.
Combing hair.
Washing extremities (arms and legs).
Bathing (bed, tub, or shower).
Drying self after bath.
Cleansing after use of toilet (bedpan, commode chair, or bathroom).
Applying deodorant.

DRESSING AND UNDRESSING

Putting on or removing —
Night clothes.
Under clothes.
Shoes and socks.
Dresses, shirts, and slacks.
Corsets, braces, "bras", prosthesis, girdles, etc.
Tying ties, fastening belts, tying shoe laces, managing buttons, zippers, etc.

EATING

Buttering bread.
Cutting meat or any food (paring or peeling).
Eating with different utensils (ability to hold the utensil).
Drinking (glass or cup) use of straw.
Passing dishes of food.
Stirring liquids.
Group eating.

HAND ACTIVITIES

Pressing signal lights or bells.
Writing.
Using telephone (holding receiver).
Sewing.
Making beds.
Dusting or cleaning rooms.
Turning lights off and on.
Lighting and smoking cigarette, cigar or pipe.
Turning pages of book, magazine, or newspaper.
Handling furniture and gadgets: drawers, doors, faucets, keys, etc.
Using reachers (from bed, wheelchair, or chair to pick up objects).
Cleaning eyeglasses.
Winding and setting watch.

WHEELCHAIR ACTIVITIES

Moving from bed to wheelchair and reverse.
Moving from wheelchair to toilet seat.
Moving from wheelchair to tub.
Moving from wheelchair to shower (stool or bench).
Rising from wheelchair to standing position.
Transferring from wheelchair to automobile.
Propelling wheelchair.
Locking wheelchair brakes.
Raising and lowering foot pedals.
Propelling wheelchair through doorways over doorsills.
Propelling wheelchair on ramps (angle of ramp).

WALKING

Moving from bed to standing position.
Rising from wheelchair or any chair to standing position.
Using cane, crutches, walkers, etc.
Going through doorways with crutches, walkers or canes.

Walking—continued

Walking on rough surfaces — loss of balance.
Climbing stairs.
Stepping up on or off of curbs.

TOILETING ACTIVITIES

Manipulating bedpan, urinal.
Manipulating clothing when using toilet stool.

PRINCIPLES

- Recognize the potential abilities of the patient and the reasons *why* he is not using these.

- Be aware that each self-care activity is made up of many individual steps and that inability to do any one of these will prevent the patient from accomplishing the activity independently.

- Bear in mind that understanding, patience, and consistency of instruction are essentials for teaching self-care.

- Allow the patient time to complete the activity without being rushed.

- Make verbal directions clear, simple, and brief.

- Learn which activity of daily living the patient is most interested in accomplishing.

- Give ADL training at the usual time of day for the activity.

- Recognize the patient's essential need for and use of good balance for independent ADL.

- Allow and encourage patient to do as much for himself as possible.

- Use adapted equipment only when absolutely necessary.

ADAPTATIONS

The following are some suggestions which may be used and adapted according to individual patient's needs. Success for the patient depends largely upon the inventiveness of both the nursing personnel and the patient himself. There are generally no standard procedures of ADL for these patients; however, the following adaptations for specific problems may prove helpful.

Limited Range of Motion

DRESSING

Recommended styles —
Larger size clothing, made of materials which have some stretch.
Adapted styles of clothing.
Larger buttons or zippers with a loop on the pull tab.
Recommended equipment —
Buttonhook may be helpful in buttoning.
Reaching tongs of all types.
Long shoehorn.
Elastic shoelaces.
Stocking aids:
- Garters attached to string.
- Garters sewed on metal loop at end of long handle.
- Garters sewed on wooden hoop at end of straps.
- Commercial aids.

Tabs sewed on clothing to facilitate use of hook on a long handle.
Mesh stockings are sometimes recommended for women.
Velcro fasteners.

FEEDING

Recommended equipment —
Built-up handles on utensils.
Elongated handles.
Plastic straw if ROM is limited in shoulder and picking up a glass or cup is difficult.
Plate guard or food stopper.

HYGIENE AND GROOMING

Recommended equipment —
Portable spray for bathing or for shampooing hair.
Reachers to hold washcloth, powder puff, etc.
Long handled combs, toothbrush.
Long lipstick.
Long handled bath brush with soap container in brush.
Extended handle for safety or electric razor.
Spray type deodorant.
Extended or built-up handles on water faucets.

Incoordination

DRESSING

Recommended styles —
Large buttons, or loops attached to pull tabs on zipper.
Buttoners or buttonhooks.
Elastic shoelaces.
Trousers with elastic tops.

FEEDING

Recommended equipment —
Suction bases for holding dishes.
Plastic straws to eliminate spilling.
Plastic drinking glasses with lids.
Weighted utensils.
Plate guards to facilitate getting food on fork.
Spork (combination spoon-fork).

HAND ACTIVITIES

Recommended equipment —
Weighted pencils.
Weighted checkers.

HYGIENE AND GROOMING

Recommended equipment —
Rubber spool curlers may be easiest to manage.
Utensils attached to string if patient has tendency to drop articles.
Suction-cup hand brushes.
Soap bar attached to a cord around the neck for bathing.
Nail file taped down to a flat surface for filing nails.

Impaired Vision

Specific principles for teaching patients with impaired vision —

- Emphasize the use of patient's sense of touch.
- Provide "landmarks" to aid patient in determining top from bottom, right from left, etc.
- Keep clothing, personal items, etc., in a definitely planned place.

DRESSING

Recommended equipment —

Piece of textured material unlike the garment material sewed to right *or* left sleeve, back of neck and back of pants. The placement should be consistent on all of patient's clothes.

Alternate method for those who have partial vision: a colored thread or piece of material attached as above.

FEEDING

Procedure —

Teach patient where the food is placed by reference to the hours on a clock face; i.e., meat at 2 o'clock, vegetables at 4 o'clock. Be consistent as to food placement.

Teach patient to use a piece of bread as a guard against which he can scoop the food onto the eating utensil.

Quadriplegics

DRESSING

Recommended styles —

Zippers or snaps in long side seams of trousers.

Blouses cut with extra length to prevent pulling out from skirt waistband.

Velcro fasteners.

Loops on trouser waistband.

FEEDING

Recommended equipment —

Leather cuff to hold fork or spoon.

Spork.

Swivel spoon, with or without stops.

Plate guard for aid in getting food on spoon.

Suction cup to hold plate.

Long plastic straw.

GROOMING

Recommended equipment —

Leather cuff to hold razor, toothbrush, comb, etc.

MINOR ACTIVITIES

Recommended equipment —

Robot smoker.

Electric page turners.

Mouth stick for turning pages, painting, typing, writing, dialing telephone, etc.

Leather cuff to hold attachments for typing, writing, and painting.

Paraplegics

DRESSING TECHNIQUES

In general, clothing is put on in the following order — under garments, stockings, braces, trousers, shoes, and shirt or dress.

Men's trousers, shorts, and women's slacks and underwear.

Recommended styles —
Slacks are easier to fasten if they button or zip down the front. In some instances slacks with long zippers in the side seams are easier to pull over braces.

Procedure —
Patient sits on bed and pulls his knees into a flexed position.
Holding the top of trousers, he flips trousers to his feet.
He works pants legs over his feet and pulls pants up to his hips.
In a semi-reclining position, he rolls from hip to hip and pulls the garment up over hips.

Comments —
Reaching tongs are sometimes necessary and useful.

Stockings

Recommended styles —
Stockings with tight elastic bands should be avoided.
Service weight nylons are recommended for women.
Stretch socks are sometimes recommended for a smooth fit.

Procedure —
While sitting on bed, patient flexes knee with one hand and slips stocking on with other hand.

Comments —
Stockings should fit smoothly since any wrinkles may cause pressure areas.
Reaching tongs are sometimes indicated.

Slips and Skirts

Recommended styles —
Slips a size or two larger than usually worn.
Full skirts for ease in pulling over hips and for better appearance over braces.

Procedure —
Patient sits on bed, slips garment over head and lets it drop to waist. In a semi-reclining position, she rolls from hip to hip and pulls the garment down over the hips and thighs.

Shoes

Recommended styles —
Shoes should fit well and offer firm support.

Procedure —

- Method I: In sitting position on bed, patient pulls one knee at a time into flexed position with his hands. While supporting leg in flexed position with one hand, he uses the free hand to put on shoe.

- Method II: Patient sits on edge of bed, or in wheelchair for back support. He crosses one leg over the other and slips shoe on.

Shirts, pajama jackets, robes, and dresses opening completely down the front.

Recommended styles —
Wrinkle-resistant, smooth, durable material.
Action-back blouses, roomy sleeves, full skirts which slip easily over the hips.

Procedure —

- Patient may balance body by putting palms of hands alternately on mattress on either side of body.

- If balance is poor, he may be given assistance or the bed backrest may be elevated. (If backrest cannot be elevated, one or two pillows may be used to support the back.) With backrest elevated, both hands are free.

- Method of putting clothing on does not usually create a problem; however, if difficulty is encountered the following method is suggested: With garments open on the lap, collar toward patient's chest, put arms into sleeves and pull up over elbows. Then, holding on to the shirttail or back of dress, pull over head, adjust and button.

Hygiene and Grooming

Recommended Equipment —
Spray hose for bathing. (Patient should keep a finger over the spray to detect sudden temperature changes in water.)
Long handled bath brushes with soap insert for ease in reaching all parts of the body.
Soap bars attached to a cord around the neck.
Wheelchair covered with a sheet of plastic for sponge bath in chair.

Skin Care

Adequate care of the skin is important in the prevention of pressure areas (redness of the skin due to a part of the body bearing its weight in one position for too long a time) and prevention of bedsores. Skin care is the *responsibility* of the *nursing* personnel.

RULES FOR SKIN CARE

- Keep patient clean and dry — of prime importance in skin care.
- Use oil or lotion, preferably one containing lanolin, for lubricating dry skin.
- Include inspection of patient's skin in the daily routine. Watch for —
    Irritation and chafing due to bed linen, braces, and clothing.
    Redness, particularly at pressure areas on bony parts of the body.
    Dryness of the skin, especially of the feet, elbows, and mouth.
- Do not allow patient to remain in any one position for a prolonged period of time as this contributes to pressure areas. Change patient's position at least every 2 hours or more often if patient's condition warrants.
- See that patient who is in a wheelchair or chair for several hours has a change of position. Periodic walks or rising to a standing position will give the necessary change.
- Encourage patient to stand whenever possible, using the foot of the bed, crutches, parallel bars, back of chair, wallbars, etc., for support when necessary. Standing stimulates circulation to legs and feet and helps prevent bedsores by relieving pressure areas.
- Make sure patient has proper bed positioning and body alignment to prevent pressure areas and deformities.
- Emphasize importance of bowel and bladder control in preventing pressure sores. A wet bed causes chafing and redness to the skin.
- Thoroughly clean incontinent patient with soap and water to prevent odors, chafing and bedsores.
- Keep linens clean, dry, and free from wrinkles and crumbs that may cause skin irritation.
- Avoid using rubber rings and "doughnuts" as they tend to lessen the circulation and cause other pressure areas.
- A diet containing the essential nutritional elements is basic to good skin condition.
- Look for signs of potential bedsores before patient reports discomfort; the skin of the older person may have reduced sensitivity.
- Examine the area and begin preventive care immediately when patient complains of a sore back, heel, or any other area where there is pressure.

Personal Hygiene

Cleanliness and a neat appearance are just as important to the patient as they are to the nurse. The nurse is responsible for assisting the patient to keep himself clean and attractive. To do this, the nurse must have a good understanding why cleanliness is so important to the patient's welfare.

Personal hygiene serves an important purpose in rehabilitation in addition to that of cleanliness. The tasks the patient performs in personal hygiene are a part of self-care, an activity that works toward independence, and by doing as much of his personal care as he is able to, the patient uses his exercises and increases his strength.

OBJECTIVES

- To aid the patient in developing good health habits in bathing, oral hygiene, and the care of fingernails and toenails.
- To improve the patient's morale and give him a sense of well-being.
- To stimulate the patient's pride in his personal appearance.

BATHING

The elderly patient should not take baths too frequently because his skin tends to be dry. However, his bath should be a pleasant experience. How often he takes a bath should be determined by his needs, but he should bathe thoroughly at least once or twice a week.

SHOWER BATHS

- A shower stall is usually easier than a tub for the older patient to use.
- A chair or a bench may be used inside the shower stall to allow the patient to sit while taking his shower.
- A wheelchair patient may be transferred onto a shower chair, thereby extending this means of bathing to a larger number of patients.
- Water temperature should always be checked closely and regulated so that it feels comfortable to the inside of the nurse's wrist. This is done to avoid burning the patient, as the older patient may have lost skin sensitivity and may be burned easily.
- Shower baths may be strange and unheard of to some patients. Always try to avert a patient's fear by showing him the shower, explaining how it works, and assuring him that you (the nurse) will be there to help him.

TUB BATHS

- Many patients are used to tub baths, but usually need help in getting in and out of the tub so that they do not fall.

- Grab rails should always be available near the tub so that the patient will have something to grasp while getting in and out of the tub.

BED BATHS

- Encourage the use of tub or shower instead of bed baths.

- If bed baths must be given, have patient do as much of his own bathing as he can.

Oral Hygiene

- Oral hygiene (cleaning and care of the mouth) should be done morning and night.

- The patient should be taught to care for his own mouth and teeth, if at all possible.

- Dentures, as well as patient's own teeth, should be carefully cleaned as they become very foul smelling and soiled when neglected. If the patient cannot or will not devote this care to his dentures, it should be done for him.

Care of the Nails

- Patient's hands and feet should be cared for. This is important for the patient's comfort as well as for his health.

- Hands and feet should be kept clean.

- Nails should be cared for at regular intervals, at least once a month; however, a check for hangnails and sharp corners or points on nails should be made daily.

- Hands and feet should be soaked in warm, soapy water before the nails are trimmed. Remember warm, not hot, water should be used because many older people have experienced a loss of feeling for extreme temperatures to the hands and feet.

- Nails should be cut straight across and not too short. A blunt scissors should be used for cutting and an emery board for filing so that underlying tissues are not injured.

Care of the Hair

- Shampoos should be given at regular intervals, at least once a month, and according to patient's need.

- Women should be given attractive hair styles to stimulate pride in personal appearance.

- Men should be shaved daily, also as a stimulus to pride in appearance.

- Hair combing and shaving should be a part of the morning care routine, and patients should be encouraged to do this for themselves whenever possible.

Clothing

- Clothing should always be kept clean and attractive.

- Patients should not be kept in pajamas and robes during the day.

- The wearing of dresses, shirts, trousers, and shoes should be encouraged.

- A change of clothing depends upon the patient's needs, but clothing should be changed at least twice a week.

- Clothing should be comfortable and of a type that patients are able to put on themselves; for example, loose fitting clothing, and dresses that open down the front.

- Care should be taken to see that the circulation to any part of the body is not hindered; for example, rolled leg garters which lessen circulation to the legs and feet should be avoided. For those who do not wear a girdle or something similar, a garter belt can be used (either bought or homemade).

Guide to Self-Care

Although patients should help themselves as much as possible, remember to instruct the patients *how* to do self-care. Encourage them to do as much as they can, and praise the patients for their attempts and progress.

BATHROOM CARE

- Take the patient into the bathroom to wash at the basin or encourage him to go to the bathroom himself if he is able rather than washing at the bedside table.

- Allow the patient to take his time.

- Encourage the patient to wash himself and to use a deodorant. A deodorant may be something entirely new to the patient so explain the reason for its use.

- Have the patient take care of his oral hygiene at this time as it is easier and safer for him to clean his dentures while at the basin.

- Encourage the male patient to shave himself or give him assistance if needed. The patient should have and use his own mirror and razor, whether an electric or a safety razor. If this is not possible, use an adequate disinfection procedure between patients.

SPONGE BATH AT THE BEDSIDE

- See that the patient is in a comfortable position in bed or is sitting at the side of the bed.

- Encourage and assist the patient to wash himself as much as he is able to.

- Supervise oral hygiene, hair combing, and dressing and give assistance only when necessary.

Bowel and Bladder Training

INCONTINENCE

Incontinence is the loss of control of either bowel or bladder or both. Some of the common causes of incontinence are spinal cord injury, disease, infection, loss of sphincter (muscle) power, loss of bladder tone, disorientation due to drugs, or lack of interest on the part of the patient or nurse in maintaining or establishing control.

PATIENT ATTITUDES

Patients may display a variety of emotions or behavior as a result of the loss of bladder and bowel control. Some of the most common behavior symptoms are nervousness, embarrassment, disgust, anger, feelings of rejection and shame. Other patients may show a complete lack of interest or seem to use their incontinence as a means of getting attention.

NURSE ATTITUDES

The nurse must show sympathy and understanding toward the patient and a great deal of patience, tact, and persistence. Giving constant encouragement or simply extending hope that it is possible to overcome his bowel and bladder problem may be enough to gain a patient's confidence and cooperation. Remember that this relearning of control is a long process and a difficult one at times.

OBJECTIVES

The two major objectives of a bowel and bladder program for the individual patient are: (1) To help in the establishment of a pattern for control of bowel and bladder functioning, and (2) To prevent urinary and bowel incontinence, thereby obtaining greater independence for the patient.

Suggested Procedure for Bowel and Bladder Routines

Each patient needs careful and complete medical evaluation to determine whether there are physical causes contributing to the incontinence. There may also be social and emotional factors present which need evaluation. The bowel and bladder program must be carefully explained to the patient including the reasons for it and the results expected which will benefit him as an individual. Additional effort by the nursing personnel to motivate the patient will undoubtedly be necessary.

The plan and procedure must be explained to the nursing personnel. Motivation may be needed for this group as well as for the patient.

All of the following factors must be considered of equal importance in working out a program for an individual patient. Any program for establishing a pattern for control of bowel and bladder requires the support and cooperation of nurses on all shifts.

Water. Liquids should be offered frequently as most older people do not drink a sufficient amount of water. Drinking water is very important for better function of both bowel and bladder. Simple constipation can be reduced by merely drinking water.

Position. Correct toilet position is of prime importance.

- The correct or normal position is a sitting position. A sitting position aids in emptying the bladder or colon as completely as possible, thus lessening incontinence.
- Using a toilet is better than using a commode chair. When toilets or commode chairs are not available, improvise by placing a bedpan on a straight chair.
- Patients using bedpans in bed should be placed in a sitting position. Patients using a bedpan while they are lying flat in bed *do not* empty their bladder and lower bowel completely.

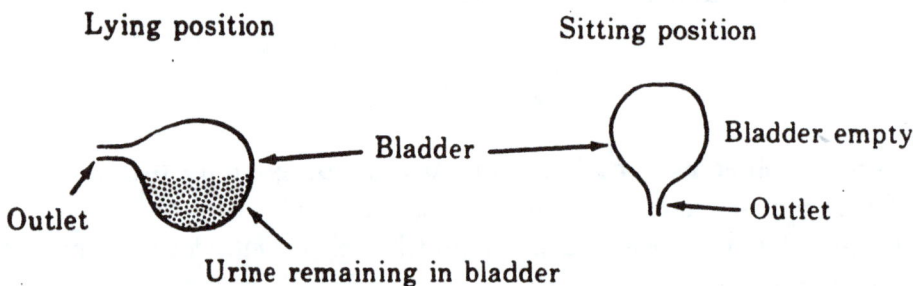

Scheduling. Patients should be taken to the bathroom to use the toilet, assisted to a commode, or given the bedpan on a scheduled basis.

- Planning a schedule should be done by all of the nurses on all three shifts in order to cover the 24-hour period.
- Scheduling must be carried out on a daily 24-hour basis at regular intervals. The

Scheduling—continued

recommended schedule is every 2 hours as a beginning and an increase to 3 and 4 hours as the plan progresses.

- Patients may need the physical assistance of the nursing personnel in going to the toilet.
- It is the nurse's responsibility to see that the patient follows the schedule, explaining to the patient the necessity of maintaining the intervals.
- Scheduling offers the patient security, and aids him in establishing a pattern.

Physical Activity. Physical activity helps stimulate bowel and bladder function and establish regularity. Whenever possible, patients should be transferred from the bed to a chair or commode or taken to the bathroom in a wheelchair to use the toilet.

Mental Activity. Recreational activities also support nursing procedures by giving patients things to do to occupy their time and minds or in giving them something to look forward to, as well as a reason for trying to establish control. Helping patients to focus their attention on something other than themselves is a tremendous aid in working toward improved bowel and bladder control.

Diet. It is of prime importance that the older person have an adequate diet containing the essential nutritional elements. This contributes to better elimination.

Patient's Normal Pattern. If the normal pattern of the patient can be learned from either the patient or his family, it should be considered in determining the schedule for the individual patient.

Time to Begin. All of the factors contributing to the problem of incontinence with the patient must be considered before determining when the chance for success seems greatest. This is the time to begin the program for control.

OTHER FACTORS TO BE CONSIDERED

Dentures. Other factors that should be considered are proper nutrition and the use of dentures when available. Using dentures allows for the proper chewing and mixing of foods. This aids in digestion, absorption, and elimination.

Laxatives and Enemas. The daily use of laxatives and enemas should be discouraged in order to avoid the laxative and enema habit. The use of laxatives and enemas does not allow the bowel to empty under its own power. It is desirable to encourage normal bowel functioning, and this can best be accomplished through the combined use of exercise, adequate diet, and regularity in bowel habits.

Mechanical Devices. Mechanical devices such as urinal bags, shower caps (filled with absorbent gauze), pads, and pants may prevent irritation and redness and decrease the amount of soiled linen. It is important to see that all devices, such as male urinal bags, fit the patient and that they are kept clean by frequent washing.